A Bully Father

Theodore Roosevelt's Letters to His Children

RANDOM HOUSE
New York

A
BULLY
FATHER

With a Biographical Essay and Notes by

Joan Paterson Kerr

Foreword by David McCullough

FRONTISPIECE: SAGAMORE HILL IN A 1904 PHOTOGRAPH BY EDWARD S. CURTIS
(Library Of Congress)

Theodore Roosevelt's letters were originally published in *Letters of Theodore Roosevelt to His Children* (Scribners, 1919).

Library of Congress Cataloging-in-Publication Data

Roosevelt, Theodore, 1858–1919.
A bully father: Theodore Roosevelt's letters to his children /
with a biographical essay and notes by Joan Paterson Kerr; foreword
by David McCullough.
p.   cm.
ISBN 0-679-43948-X (hardcover)
I. Roosevelt, Theodore, 1858–1919—Correspondence.   2. Roosevelt,
Theodore, 1858–1919—Family.   3. Roosevelt family—Correspondence.
4. Presidents—United States—Correspondence.   5. Presidents—United
States—Family relationships.   I. Kerr, Joan Paterson.   II. Title.
E757.A4   1995b
973.91′1′092—dc20   95-8585
[B]

Manufactured in the United States of America
4689753

Book design by Lilly Langotsky

For Chester,
veteran father and grandfather,
and
for Tony,
newcomer to parenthood

CAST OF CHARACTERS

*I*n the summer of 1902, during the first year the Theodore Roosevelt family occupied the White House and despite the president's determination to shield his six children from the scrutiny of the press, Frances Benjamin Johnston was given permission to photograph the family at the urging of TR's old friend, journalist Jacob Riis. Her photographs appeared in the August issue of the *Ladies' Home Journal.* True to form, when Johnston arrived at the house none of the children could be found. "Miss Alice . . . finally located them for me under their beds," the photographer recalled.

TR and Edith

Alice

Ted

Kermit

Ethel

Archie

Quentin

Auntie Bye &
Sheffield

Mame & Quentin

Contents

Foreword

by

David McCullough

"Get action!" "Seize the moment!" "Whatever you do, enjoy it!" his own father had said, and Theodore Roosevelt took him at his word, packing more into one life than any ten men of average metabolism and enjoying just about all of it all of the time. Incapable of doing anything by half measure, he embraced every part he ever played—scholar, suitor, soldier, cowboy and bear-hunter, husband, politician, president of the United States—but that of being a father most especially. He took on the role for his six children as if life depended on it, his and theirs.

He wanted to be all that his own father had been for him, and then some. He adored children. He adored the whole time of life called childhood, and as Joan Paterson Kerr writes in the delightful pages that follow, he had no intention of hastening his children out of childhood.

But then it may also be said neither did Theodore Roosevelt himself wish ever to depart that blessed state any sooner than necessary. The youngest of our presidents in fact, he remained the youngest in spirit as well. He was exuberantly fond of any number and variety of household pets. He joined in pillow fights, picnics, relished ghost stories in the dark, bedtime stories, stories of any kind.

"You must always remember," observed his friend Cecil Spring Rice, the British diplomat, "that the President is about six."

Nothing, not the experience of war or the death of loved ones, not the passing of years or the burdens of high office, could extinguish, even subdue for long, the ardent vitality and imagination of the child within. Years after leaving the White House, in explanation of an extremely hazardous, ill-advised exploring expedition to Brazil that he took part in, he said simply, "I had to go. It was my last chance to be a boy again."

He was the kind of father who, at the dinner table, would serve the youngest child first, or who, when their mother was not looking, would cut the icing off his own cake and slip it to the nearest child. A baby's hand, he thought, was the most beautiful of God's creations.

"I love all these children and have great fun with them," he wrote to his sister-in-law, in a letter included here, "and I am touched by the way in which they feel I am their special friend, champion and companion." If separated from them, he wanted them to know they were never out of mind. To be sure they knew his feelings, he poured himself out on paper in some of the most engaging letters ever written by an American father, let alone a president of the United States, busy as he was. Full of news, advice, opinion, always full of affection, the letters can be seen now as child support of another kind from another era.

Some he illustrated with his own memorable line drawings, knowing perfectly what pleasure these would give. More often, it is his talent for the vivid word picture that makes what he wrote so exceptional. There is the letter of November 20, 1906, describing for young Ted what he saw on his famous trip to Panama. I know of no better eyewitness portrayal of the great tumult of the steam shovels at work in Cuelbra Cut.

A noted latter-day child psychologist, Margaret McPharland, liked to stress that attitudes aren't taught, they're caught. Certainly among the prevailing attitudes to be caught from Theodore Roosevelt's letters to his children is that life is infinitely interesting and that the more interest we take, the more fun it becomes. He writes of history, health, his horse, his travels, keelboats on the Mississippi, books, art, Africa at night, not to mention the doings of others in the family. The characters in Dickens, he offers, "are really to a great degree personified attributes rather than individuals." The mysteries of mental telepathy are no light matter, for after all "there is much in it and in kindred things which are real and which at present we do not understand."

There is never doubt of his love for each of the children, his trust in them, his devotion to their mother, or that home is where his heart is. "After all, fond as I am of the White House, there isn't any place in the world like home—like Sagamore Hill, where things are our own, with our own associations, and where it is really country."

Spanning a dozen years, from 1898 to 1911, the letters come to us from that vanished day when family correspondence was still an established part of family life, and when letters were written not just to be read but read aloud. They were family talk on paper, and for the voluble Roosevelts, who seldom ever stopped talking, this was particularly so. It is a point for the modern reader to bear in mind for the full enjoyment of the letters.

There are, for example, two accounts by the president of the

United States of his slam-bang encounters at the White House with a couple of Japanese wrestlers, in letters to sons Kermit and Ted, which clearly were written for their hilarious effect when delivered aloud. Almost a century later, at the invitation of President Bush to speak about TR at the White House, I read these same letters in the course of my talk and with exactly the result their author intended.

Theodore Roosevelt did not live to see his face on Mount Rushmore or his conservation ethic enter into the mainstream of American politics as it has in our time. Nor did he live to see his letters to his children appear in book form, first in 1919. But the impress of his personality is to be found here as much as anywhere, and of the more than twenty books he wrote, this is the most charming, the most expressive of the warmth that made him so endearing to those closest to him.

Further, with the issue of American family life so in the forefront now, with the very survival of the family as the keystone of American society in question as never before, this new edition of the letters could not be more timely or valuable. And with it comes the bonus of Joan Paterson Kerr's fine family chronicle, which even after all these years contains new information—including TR's letters to Alice, a diary kept by Alice when she was sixteen, a ghost story often told by TR around the campfire—plus an album's worth of family photographs.

Roosevelt often said that if he enjoyed a particular book, he would come back to it again and again, always finding something new in it, or in himself. This, I'm sure, will be just such a book for many readers for many years to come.

A Bully Father

ORIGINS OF
FATHERHOOD

Theodore Roosevelt, twenty-sixth president of the United States and father of six, was the quintessential family man. In letter after letter that he wrote to his family and friends, he spoke of the pride, the love, and the joy that he derived from his family. No matter that he had achieved the highest position in the land, his wife and children came first. He was indeed a "bully" father. This was a word he often used to describe having a wonderful time and, in its most famous usage, the way he looked at the presidency as "a bully pulpit." In 1904, when he had just been elected president by an overwhelming majority, he wrote to his son Kermit that "it was a great comfort to feel, all during the last days when affairs looked doubtful, that no matter how things came out the really important thing was the lovely life I have with mother and with you children and that compared to this home life everything else was of very small importance from the standpoint of happiness." He had written similarly to his sister, Bamie, that if defeated he would be disappointed, but infinitely more important, he declared, was the fact that he had had "the happiest home life of any man whom I have ever known."

Such remarkable devotion to family had its roots in TR's own upbringing. He himself had been one of four children; a sister Anna, called Bamie or Bye, born in 1855 and almost four years his senior; a brother Elliott, or Ellie, a year and a half younger, and Corinne, or Conie, the baby of the family. He was known as "Teedie." His was an extraordinarily close-knit family, one that believed in showing affection openly and frequently. His mother called their uninhibited embraces "melts." When Teedie went away to college for his first long separation from his family, he wrote home to his "Beloved Motherling" that he hardly knew a boy "who is on as intimate and affectionate terms with his family as I am."

Teedie's mother, Martha Bulloch, known as "Mittie," was, according to her eldest son, "a sweet, gracious, beautiful Southern woman, a delightful companion and beloved by everybody." Her romantic and adventurous family from Georgia were totally different from the staid and proper Dutch Roosevelts, true New York Knickerbockers. Mittie's relatives followed paths that held high drama for Teedie. One uncle, James Bulloch, an admiral in the Confederate navy, was the builder of the famous Confederate war vessel *Alabama.* Another uncle, Irvine Bulloch, was a midshipman on the *Alabama,* "and fired the last gun discharged from her batteries in the fight with the *Kearsarge,*" Teedie was told.

Mittie's Southern heritage created a major and cruel problem for the Roosevelt family when the Civil War split the country apart. Unwilling to fight against Mittie's brothers, Teedie's father declined active duty in the Union forces, a position with which his young son never quite came to terms, or so his daughter Alice thought.

Teedie adored his father and with good reason. A strikingly handsome man, a physical attribute that his namesake did not inherit, the elder Theodore combined his business career as a partner in the importing firm of Roosevelt & Son with numerous charitable and philanthropic activities. He was a founder not only of the Children's Aid Society, the New York Orthopedic Hospital, and the Newsboys' Lodging House among others, but of the American Museum of Natural History and the Metropolitan Museum of Art as well. At the time of Teedie's birth he was twenty-seven years old, financially secure, and already one of New York's leading citizens. But it was his winsome personality that endeared him to his children. Writing of him later in life to a friend, Teedie flatly stated, "I was fortunate enough in having a father whom I have always been able to regard as an ideal man."

At the age of three Teedie had begun to suffer from asthmatic attacks of such severity that when the usual palliatives of the day such as coffee, ipecac, or tobacco failed to work, the elder Theodore would bundle the child up in heavy garments, summon the groom and carriage, and dash through the cold, dark streets of New York hoping to force air into Teedie's heaving lungs. Years later Teedie recalled with grateful affection that "the thought of him now and always has been a sense of comfort. I could breathe, I could sleep, when he had me in his arms. My father—he got me breath, he got me lungs, strength—life."

"Theodore," his father told him when he was about twelve, "you have the mind but you have not the body, and without the help of the body the mind cannot go as far as it should. You must *make* your body. It is hard drudgery to make one's body but I know you will do it."

Young Teedie agreed to try. His parents then turned a second-story piazza of their house on Twentieth Street in New York City into an open air gymnasium and filled it with parallel and swinging bars, ladders, and other forms of athletic paraphernalia.

Having accepted his father's challenge, Teedie diligently began daily workouts, "widening his chest by regular monotonous motion—drudgery indeed," Conie remembered.

Vacation sites were chosen to enable long days breathing country air, and summers generally lasted from early June until late September. "We children, of course, loved the country beyond anything," TR recalled. "We disliked the city. We were always wildly eager to get to the country when spring came, and very sad when in the late fall the family moved back to town." Teedie's health began to improve.

The country also provided Teedie with the laboratory he needed to indulge his passion for natural history. As a small boy he had started a collection of specimens in his room, which he soon was ambitiously calling the "Roosevelt Museum of Natural History." When he was thirteen, he was allowed to take lessons in taxidermy; he was also given his first gun. More important, he discovered he could not see to shoot like other boys and was provided, at long last, with spectacles, "which literally opened an entirely new world" to him. He seriously considered making science his life's work.

In 1874, when Teedie was sixteen, his father rented a gracious, white-pillared house at Oyster Bay on Long Island's North Shore, joining the colony there that had been started by his family. There were morning horseback rides, tramps through the woods, walks to nearby beaches that lured the swimmer into the sparkling waters of Long Island Sound, and family picnics all organized by Father just as TR would do a decade later when he built his own home close by on Cove Neck Road. "There could be no healthier and pleasanter place to bring up children than in that nook of old-time America," TR believed. Like his father before him, TR felt that giving children liberty in the summertime was an unparalleled way to stimulate their imaginations. He also took delight in following his father's advice and urging his children to do likewise: "Whatever you do, enjoy it."

The Christmases "of literally delirious joy" that his parents provided their children TR would later imitate step by step for his own family. Stockings, the biggest they could borrow from the grownups, were hung up in the evening on the fireplace in their parents' room, and before dawn Bamie, Teedie, Ellie, and Conie would troop in and open them sitting on their mother and father's bed. After breakfast the doors to the drawing room were flung open and each child raced to his own table, on which the bigger presents had been placed. "I never knew any one else to have what seemed to me such attractive Christmases," TR recalled, "and in the next generation I tried to reproduce them exactly for my own children."

He felt the same way about the custom of going to his father's room while he was dressing to examine anything that came out of his pockets, and in the little box on his dressing table where he used to keep trinkets, which the children called "treasures." That word, and some of the trinkets themselves, passed on to the next generation. TR recounted that his own children, when small, "used to troop into my room while I was dressing, and the gradually accumulating trinkets in the 'ditty box'—the gift of an enlisted man in the navy—always excited rapturous joy."

When Theodore senior died in 1877 at the age of forty-six, TR, then in his second year at Harvard, was completely undone. He had written his father shortly after he had entered college that "I do not think there is a fellow in College who has a family that love him as much as you all do me, and I am *sure* that there is no one who has a Father who is also his best and most intimate friend, as you are mine."

In October 1901, he recounted much of this to an old family
friend who had congratulated him on becoming president.

Dear Mrs. Leavitt,

I knew I should hear from you and I loved your letter. Yes,
I have thought of father all the time and of how pleased he
would be: what would I not give if only he could have lived
until now and seen me here in the White House, and all his
grandchildren, and everything! . . .

Do you know that at the end of my term here, in 1905, I
shall be exactly the age father was when he died?

Unconsciously, I always find I am trying to model myself
with my children on the way he was with us.

Lovingly yours

In the fall of TR's junior year at Harvard, a friend had invited him
for a weekend at his family's home in nearby Chestnut Hill. Next
door lived Alice Hathaway Lee, one of the prettiest girls Theodore
had ever laid eyes on, and he was soon hopelessly in love. He pur-
sued her with all the vigor he brought to everything he did, pour-
ing his heart out in his diary. "She is so marvelously sweet, and pure
and loveable and pretty that I seem to love her more and more every
time I see her, though I love her so much now that I really *can not*
love her more. I do not think ever a man loved a woman more than
I love her. . . ." The Roosevelt "melts" were working full throttle as
TR exulted, "I can hold her in my arms and kiss her and caress her
and love her as much as I choose."

They were married after his graduation in the fall of 1880. TR
took her to the family house at Oyster Bay for their honeymoon,

and it was here that they began to plan their own home to be built on a nearby hill overlooking the water on three sides. It was to be called "Leeholm" after its mistress and was to have ten bedrooms, plus maids' rooms—a clue to their family expectations.

Returning to New York, TR first attended Columbia Law School but abandoned it to run for the state assembly on the Republican ticket, something very few "gentlemen" of his day considered an appropriate career choice. TR reveled in his days in the legislature and learned a number of practical lessons, one of which he later passed on to Ted junior while he was at school and dealing with a football squad of boys considerably larger and older than himself.

Dear Ted:

Your letter pleased me very much. I think your decision was wise and right. And oh, Ted! I was so much amused and interested with the description of the way you got to feel because you had won the position for yourself in the football field among the older fellows. I never did well enough in athletics while a boy to get such a position, either at school or college; but, immediately after leaving college I went to the legislature. I was the youngest man there, and I rose like a rocket. I was re-elected next year by an enormous majority in a time when the republican party as a whole met with great disaster; and the republican minority in the house, although I was the youngest member, nominated me for speaker, that is, made me the leader of the minority. I immediately proceeded to lose *my* perspective, also. Unfortunately, I did not recover it as early as you have done in this case, and the result was that I came an awful cropper and had to pick myself up after learning by bitter experience the lesson that I was not all-impor-

tant and that I had to take account of many different elements
in life. It took me fully a year before I got back the position I
had lost, but I hung steadily at it and achieved my purpose. . . .

Ever your loving father

Beyond finding political life much to his liking, TR's cup brimmed
over when Alice became pregnant in 1883. Since he stayed in
rooms in Albany during the week while the legislature was in session, he moved Alice into Mittie's large house at 6 West Fifty-sev-
enth Street, where the family had moved in 1873.

It was here that Alice Lee Roosevelt, TR's first child, was born
on February 12, 1884, under circumstances so tragic as to be almost beyond human understanding. TR had received a first
telegram announcing the birth, which was greeted with jubilation.
A second telegram a few hours later sent him rushing for the next
train, which, because of intense fog, crept toward New York at a
snail's pace. He arrived home to be met by his brother, Elliott, and
learned that not only was Alice dying, stricken by Bright's disease,
a chronic inflammation of the kidney, but his mother was also near
death from typhoid fever. Mittie died at three o'clock that morning. Alice, whom Theodore held in his arms throughout the long
ghastly night and following day, died that afternoon. Elliott spoke
for them all when he cried: "There is a curse on this house."

Theodore was devastated. Unable even to speak his wife's name,
then or ever after, he entrusted "Baby Lee" to Bamie's care, returned
to Albany, and engulfed himself in a torrent of work. Thus little
Alice, who was to have been the joy of her father's and mother's
lives and the first of many to occupy one of the ten bedrooms at
Leeholm, was "given away," as she was never to forget, while her
stricken father struggled to survive his grief.

Fortunately, Bamie was a wise and compassionate woman whose devotion to TR was total, lasting even beyond her late marriage, when she was forty, to admiral William Sheffield Cowles and the birth of her own son, Sheffield. She enveloped Alice with motherly warmth, becoming for the child, as Alice would later say, "the only one I really cared about." Auntie Bye, as all the young Roosevelts came to call her, was also the crucial link for Alice to her own mother, the one who talked to her about the sweet, pretty woman she had never known.

TR declined renomination for a fourth term in the legislature, feeling that he must get away from Albany, from New York, and from the bitter memories that hounded him. He would go back to the Badlands of the Dakota Territory, where he had invested in a small cattle ranch. There he could fill his days with long hours in the saddle, learn the rugged ways of a rancher, hunt elk and buffalo, and spend the lonely evenings at his books. "Black care rarely sits behind a rider whose pace is fast enough," he once wrote.

However, his foreman and old hunting friend from Maine, Bill Sewall, recognized TR's deep melancholia and in his rough but sympathetic way tried to cheer him. When TR told Bill he had nothing to live for, Sewall reminded him that he had his child. He never forgot TR's sad reply: "Her aunt can take care of her a good deal better than I can. She never would know anything about me, anyway. She would be just as well off without me."

Deep in his heart, TR did not really believe these words, as his frequent letters to Bamie attest. "I shall be very, very glad to see you all again; I hope Mousiekins will be very cunning; I shall dearly love her." And later, "I miss both you and darling Baby Lee dreadfully; kiss her many times for me; I am really hungry to see her. She must be just too cunning for anything." In addition, he had not abandoned his plans for Leeholm and had entrusted the saintly Bamie to supervise the house's construction in his absence. His intention was that they would spend their summers together there, with Bamie raising Baby Lee.

All in all, TR spent parts of three years in the West, returning frequently to Bamie's house and watching "Mousiekins" grow into an enchanting flaxen-haired little girl with wide-spaced eyes and a broad brow. And it was during these western years that TR experienced a set of adventures that his children never tired of hearing him recall. Among many favorites was his account of killing his first grizzly, a monster of a creature close to nine feet tall, and not more than twenty feet away when their father put a bullet "as exactly between his eyes as if I had measured the distance with a carpenter's rule." The children could verify this feat for themselves, for the skin was promptly sent back to Bamie to adorn the floor at Oyster Bay, where it was to become a soft and favorite napping place for them. Other hunting trophies followed—two more grizzly bears, six elk: "three of them have magnificent heads and will look well in the 'house on the hill.' . . . I now have a dozen good heads for the hall," he exultantly wrote to Bamie.

All four of TR's sons were to benefit from their father's western experiences, for as soon as they were capable of holding a rifle he introduced each in turn to hunting and to life in the wilderness. All four took after him in their enthusiasm for outdoor life. "I am one of those fortunate ones who had a father who took the time and made the effort to instill in his sons a love of the great outdoors," Archie wrote. "He taught us to accept the discomforts and hardships that attend sport in the open fields and wilderness, and accept them as a challenge to our manhood."

Kermit, in his book *The Happy Hunting-Grounds*, recalled that "by the time we were twelve or thirteen we were encouraged to plan hunting trips in the west. Father never had time to go with us, but we would be sent out to some friend of his, like Captain Seth Bullock, to spend two or three weeks in the Black Hills, or perhaps we would go after duck and prairie-chicken with Marvin Hewitt. Father would enter into all the plans and go down with us to the range to practice with rifle or shotgun, and when we came back we would go over every detail of the trip with him, revelling in his praise when he felt that we had acquitted ourselves well."

To TR's great pleasure, each of his sons became a skillful hunter, and indeed as R. L. Wilson pointed out in his book *Theodore Roosevelt Outdoorsman,*

The Roosevelt family's hunting record is unrivaled in the history of the pursuit of big game among American sportsmen. This holds true for their contributions to the literature of hunting. The family's all-around achievements are unique: Over fifteen books on big-game hunting, countless articles in sundry periodicals, hundreds of specimens in major museums of America and Europe, the creation of the Boone and Crockett Club and the Sagamore Hill Medal, the creation and sponsorship of effective game conservation programs, and the successful pursuit of an infinite variety of trophies on six continents. It is an unblemished record of responsible and conscientious accomplishment which has earned the respect and admiration of hunters and conservationists the world over.

On one of his visits east to Bamie and Baby Lee, TR ran into an old family friend, Edith Kermit Carow, whom he had known since childhood. During the years before young Teedie entered Harvard, he and Edith had enjoyed a close relationship, which now rekindled into a lasting love affair and an extraordinary partnership that was to sustain him for the rest of his life. He prepared to leave the West behind him.

But the influence of the West on him had been incalculable in "molding his character and stimulating his zest for action." He told a friend that if asked what experience in all his life he would choose to remember, "I would take the memory of my life on the ranch with its experiences close to Nature and among the men who lived nearest her."

Two years earlier the stricken young man had written, "And when my heart's dearest died, the light went out from my life forever." Now he was ready once again for the world he had left and for the family life he had always hoped for.

SUMMERS AT
SAGAMORE

Theodore and Edith were married quietly in London on December 2, 1886, and after a honeymoon abroad they returned home to take up residence in Oyster Bay. The large, rambling house on the hill, completed the year before, was no longer to be called Leeholm. TR changed it to "Sagamore Hill," taking the name from the old Sagamore (i.e., chieftain) Mohannis, "who, as chief of his little tribe," TR wrote in his *Autobiography*, "signed away his rights to the land two centuries and a half ago."

The great Victorian-style house was everything TR had hoped it would be. With its twenty-three rooms, gables, dormers, and verandahs, it exuded, in the words of Hermann Hagedorn in his charming book *The Roosevelt Family of Sagamore Hill*, "solidity, first of all; dignity, hospitality, comfort, the social stability of the owner, and permanence. The foundations were twenty inches thick; joists, rafters and roofboards were in proportion. Long Island's gales were not going to shake this house. . . ."

But despite two hot-air furnaces in its cellar, the four fireplaces on the first floor and four on the second, with a dumbwaiter for firewood rising from the cellar to feed them, the house still came to be called the Bird Cage by the family, because by its very position astride the hill the blasts of winter air made it almost impossible to heat.

But TR loved the location. No other house was visible from it, and as he said, "We have no one looking into our pantry and there is no need to close a shutter." He did not "live in his neighbor's pocket."

He relished the fact that the children could run around barefoot, doing what they pleased with no neighbors to object or criticize. A reporter for *The Saturday Evening Post,* visiting Sagamore Hill in 1902, described the setting:

> There is an open space all around the house, so that it is always bathed in plenty of light and air and sunshine; behind it are great trees, oak and chestnut and hickory. In the background lies the Sound, the Bay and the opposite Connecticut shore ... a setting full of color for a panorama which is always full of motion, for Sound and Bay are dotted with boats ... the President never tires of the view.

And TR never tired of the house he had so lovingly designed. He admitted that he did not know enough to be sure of what he wished in outside matters, but there was no question in his mind about what the inside should be like, what he desired to live in and with. Years later, in a letter to the editor of *Country Life in America,* he explained:

> I wished a big piazza, very broad at the N. W. corner where we could sit in rocking chairs and look at the sunset; a library with a shallow bay window opening south; the parlor or drawing room oc-

cupying all the western end of the lower floor; as broad a hall as our space would permit; big fireplaces for logs; on the top floor the gun room occupying the western end so that north and west it looks over the sound and bay. I had to live inside and not outside the house; and while I should have liked to "express" myself in both, as I had to choose I chose the former.

Over the west entrance doorway was carved the Roosevelt family motto, *Qui plantavit curabit*—"He who has planted will preserve." This great, unstylish, sturdy house, as David McCullough so aptly discerned in his book about TR's early life, *Mornings on Horseback,* bespoke *family.* For the remainder of his life, Sagamore Hill was home.

TR had told the writer from *The Saturday Evening Post* that he wanted the house to have distinctive memories for his children; he wanted them to remember it when in later years they went out into the world. The writer observed: "It is quite certain that Sagamore Hill will always be to the Roosevelt children the one spot that will be quite different to them from any other. No matter what houses they may build for themselves, Sagamore Hill will hold in their memories an affection that can never be effaced."

In Ted junior's memoir, *All in the Family,* that affection is immediately apparent:

The house has that air of having been lived in which is the requisite of every home . . . Though the exterior of the house may be ugly, no one could call it ugly within. Sagamore is the offspring of the years as surely as is a reef of coral. Wings and rooms, pictures and furniture, have been built or bought "the year your brother Quentin was born," or "when your Father came back from Africa." Each tells a story in the same fashion as the rings in the trunk of a great tree.

Here is a footstool "from your great-grandfather's house on 14th Street." There is a rosewood desk that "belonged to your great-aunt Kermit. . . ." To understand a family it is necessary to know what their house is like, for the home where a family grows up is always a part of the background of life for every child. The beauty of the house makes surprisingly little difference to the children. It is what happens there that counts."

⌒

TR and Edith had stopped first in New York on their way home from Europe to retrieve little Alice from her Auntie Bye. "Mousiekins" had turned three on February 12, and as she had known no other parent, the parting for both was wrenching. "It almost broke my heart to give her up," Bamie wrote in a letter many years later. "Still I felt perfectly sure that it was for her good, and that unless she lived with her father she would never see much of him, and as my father and I had had such a close relationship, this would have been a terrible wrong to her, all of which fortunately proved true, as she adored her father and was really more like him than any of his other children."

Edith had returned home from her honeymoon happily pregnant, but from March until the birth of Ted junior in September of 1887, little Alice had the undivided attention of her father and her new "Mother," as Edith encouraged her to call her from the start. She made the most of her position in this triumvirate, riding imperiously on her father's back down to breakfast every morning, commanding him "with unintentional irreverence," as he wrote Bamie, "Now, pig!' " Theodore spent hours with her on the floor with her blocks, building houses and delighting her with stories of the make-believe people who inhabited them.

It had been decided that Alice would spend three weeks in the spring and fall with her maternal grandparents, George and Caroline Lee, in Boston and Chestnut Hill. She was then their only grandchild and was thoroughly spoiled by them. On her returns home she would invariably start weeping and wailing, aware that Edith felt that these visits had unsettled her for the less luxurious life of Sagamore Hill.

As the Lees were substantially better off than the young Roosevelts, they were able to give Alice a generous allowance, causing TR to joke to Edith that "We'd better be nice to Alice. We might have to ask her for money."

A few years after the visiting arrangements began, Edith wrote to her sister Emily in Italy, "I shall be glad to see Alice tomorrow. I hear she threw her arms around Mrs. Lee's neck and said, 'I have the best Grandmother and the best Mother in the world!' Thought it very sweet of the child."

But Alice was not always enthusiastic about her stepmother. In fact, her feelings for Edith were highly ambivalent. On the one hand, she felt in later life that her being the child of another marriage made a situation that had to be coped with, "and Mother coped with it with a fairness and charm and intelligence which she has to a greater degree than almost anyone I know." This was said when Edith was still alive. After her death, Alice was more blunt, admitting in conversations with Michael Teague for his book *Mrs. L* that she felt Edith had always resented being TR's second choice and that she never really forgave him his first marriage. Alice's brother Ted had also repeated to her Edith's remark that it was just as well that her mother had died when she did because her father would have been bored to death staying married to her. "In many ways she was a very hard woman," Alice felt.

If Edith had private thoughts about Alice, they stayed private. The many letters Edith wrote to her mother or sister bear testimony "to her impartial love for all the children," Hermann Hagedorn noted. "Every solicitous or playful reference to Alice indicated that her stepdaughter was no less precious to her than her own children."

There is no question that Edith made an effort over Alice. Writing to TR from Sagamore in August 1889, when Alice was five, she told him: "I am trying to make Alice more of a companion. I am afraid I do not do rightly in not adapting myself more to her. Several times I have gone to drive with the children and tried to talk to her, and this morning I invited her to help (!) me arrange the flowers. . . . I wish I were gayer for the children's sake. Alice needs someone to laugh and romp with her instead of a sober and staid person like me."

Fortunately there was Father to fill that role, and in quick succession Edith had five of her own children, just the kind of family TR had dreamed of when planning Sagamore. When Ted junior arrived on the scene, Alice placed her little rocking chair beside his crib, called him "my own little brother," described him as "a howling polly parrot," and refused to relinquish her post despite the addition to the household of Mary "Mame" Ledwith. This venerable Irish lady had been Edith's own nurse as a child and now took charge of the Roosevelts' nursery. Alice's proprietorship extended to the point that when it was time for her to make her customary fall visit to her grandparents she made clear she would not go unless she could take little Ted with her. Such devotion was amply repaid. Ted grew up adoring his older sister. At age two and a half—as recorded in a kind of scrapbook Edith kept during the children's earliest years called "The Baby's Journal"—he "was wild with joy when Alice came home (from Boston) and kept running and throwing his arms about her knees or kissing her hand. She brought him a drum and on going to bed he laid the drumsticks by his Papa's photograph that Papa might take care of them."

The birth of his first son, his namesake and heir, brought TR great joy, as well as understandable relief at Edith's quick recovery. Years later, in a letter to Ted's wife, TR fondly recalled those early days of his son's babyhood:

> How well I remember when we were fitting up our nursery for Ted! And he was such a cunning baby. . . . I can see him now, hanging on the little nursery gate and begging to be taken off to extra-nursery excitement; and if his request were granted, his arms and legs were waved with frantic jubilance as he was borne off, making him about as easy to carry as an electric starfish. Then, when he slept by us in a crib (a cradle is *far* better in the early stages) he would begin what his mother called his "hymn to the light," at dawn; and, when he was old enough, if I was unwary enough to give the least sign of being awake, he would swarm into bed with me and gleefully propose "a story," keeping a vigilant watch on me for any sign of sleepiness on my part while I told it.

Father and son hit it off from the beginning. With TR working at home on his books there was ample time for him to observe the little fellow, and it was his proud boast that Ted "plays more vigorously than anyone I ever saw." He spent hours romping with Alice and Ted, his adventurous imagination inflaming theirs.

One day he provided them with toy horses and cattle, which he marked with his own ranch brand using "a wire hairpin red hot." On another he helped them pretend to fight the Civil War battle of Mobile Bay with pasteboard models of rams and monitors. As the fight approached its climax, Alice suspected she might lose it. Father recorded her solution in his *Autobiography:*

> Alice: Brother, don't you sink my monitor!
> Ted: And the torpedo went at the monitor!
> Alice: My monitor is not to sink!
> Ted: And bang the monitor sank!
> Alice: It didn't do any such thing. My monitor always goes to bed at seven and it's now quarter past. My monitor was in bed and *couldn't* sink!

Father could always be coerced into playig hide-and-go-seek, one of the "pleasantest and most scary of games" (Alice's description). TR's role was to go to one of the dark rooms on the third floor and, when a child approached on his search, to moan and groan or growl, sending the child scuttling away and downstairs again in a state of delighted terror. Alice reported that Father used to say "that it was the most restful game for him that he could possibly imagine."

Restful was not, however, an adjective often used to describe Father. At Sagamore he invariably began his day with a long horseback ride, accompanied whenever possible by Edith and his children, as one by one they grew big enough to get their legs around a fat Shetland pony. In the early days he was an enthusiastic polo player, finding "a stiff polo match rather good exercise" for "a corpulent middle-aged literary man." Oblivious to danger, he rode to hounds with Long Island's Meadowbrook Hunt, one of the roughest in the country with jumps often five feet and over. When Alice was a tiny tot, she used to wait for him at the stable door. After one particularly harrowing hunt, he arrived home "looking like the walls of a slaughter-house." His horse had stumbled going over a wall, pitching him into a pile of stones, lacerating his face and breaking his arm. Little Alice, terrified by the blood and dangling arm, ran screaming to the house.

But in the spring of 1889 Father's life as author and energetic country squire at Sagamore Hill was abruptly changed when President Benjamin Harrison appointed him to the Civil Service Commission in Washington.

Edith was pregnant again, and it was decided that she would remain in the country until after the birth of the baby. TR was therefore in the capital when Kermit arrived unexpectedly early in October. The frantic father rushed home, but he missed his ferry connection from New York to Long Island City and the last train from there to Oyster Bay. Father chartered a special train at the Long Island City depot to get him home as fast as possible. He arrived at Sagamore Hill at four o'clock in the morning to find Bamie, who had been summoned, in full charge and mother and son doing well.

Kermit was a frail baby, pale with yellow hair, relatively slow in his mental development compared with Ted at his age, in his mother's opinion, but "a darling little fellow, so soft and sweet" to his father's eyes. His frailness was a matter of concern to Mame as well as his mother. He had very little appetite, so the devoted and seasoned nurse enticed him to eat meat by calling steaks "tender lion." When he was about four and feeling a little under the weather, his father saw him coming downstairs to go out in the pony cart with the fat, bored pony General Grant. He was clutching Mame's dress, and as his father reported to Edith's mother, Grandmother Carow, he kept saying, "I know Fader will lend 'ee tall umbrella to a poor sick boy." Although there was not a cloud in the sky, Father did not have the heart to refuse this "regular little coax." He described how he and Kermit would play hide-and-go-seek together, "a seemingly rapturous joy to him, but certainly a game of phenomenal tameness, played in this fashion; he buries his curly head in a sofa cushion, and calls out 'go hide your eyes, Fader!' which means, not that I am to hide my eyes, but go and hide. So I select a somewhat open hiding place and begin to 'coop'; and even so he never finds me unless I keep up a rapid succession of noises which would do no discredit to an amateur foghorn."

From the start, Kermit developed an intense affection for his Mamma. Archie Butt, TR's young military aide during his presidency, noticed that whenever Kermit stood near his mother, it was always with an arm around her waist and that he never came into a room she was in without going up and kissing her.

Little Ted, on the other hand, was decidedly his father's boy. When he was three and a half, Mame overheard him talking to himself in his bed just before his Papa was due home. "A nice little moustache, and white teeth, and black hair, very short and a nice smell of cologne, and wears glasses and gray trousers—nice gray trousers, and white feet with bones in them and red slippers, and that's my Papa."

Not long after that, Ted too started wearing big spectacles, making him look more like a "Paddy Brownie" than ever. But also more like his father, which was what he most desired. One night when Alice and Ted would not quiet down, Mame threatened to call their father and Ted agreed that she should "call Misser Roosevelt." When Alice called him a little goose for not knowing that Mr. Roosevelt was Papa, Ted happily replied, "Ted is Misser Roosevelt too!" But then, stricken, he recognized he was not an exact replica: "But Ted got no mufstache! Oh Mame, Mame, Ted got nuffin but a mouf!"

TR loved the enthusiastic reception Ted gave him after every absence but acknowledged that it might have something to do with Ted's awareness that Father was sure to have a large bundle of toys with him. He would ask his father, "Fats in de bag?" while he danced around him like an expectant little bear. Ted was inclined to the belief that toys were not possible without Papa. When Edith returned from a month's trip to TR's ranch, having left the three young children at Sagamore, she reported that they had discussed with much interest whether Mamma would bring them toys. Ted had flatly declared that "Papa will come too. Papa will say to Mamma, 'Wait a minute, Edie. I will come and bring the toys.'"

As the children grew bigger and stronger, Father devised more adventurous activities for them. He would take his "bunnies," as he now began to refer to them, on walks down to the old barn to feed the ponies and see the chickens, or to the pond, where they were made to walk out on a half-sunken log where they "perched like so-many sand-snipe."

In the evening there were wild romps, with Father usually assuming the role of a "very big bear" while the children were the little bears or raccoons or badgers. TR admitted that some child was invariably "fearfully damaged" in the play, but this did not seem to affect the ardor of anyone's enjoyment. However, these romps often led to nightmares, and Mother decreed that they could only be indulged in well before supper. In this, as always, Father meekly obeyed. But the romps became a fixture in the daily routine, looked forward to with the greatest anticipation.

During afternoon tea, as Ted and Alice hovered around his chair, Father was adept at surreptitiously giving them all the icing off his cake, provided Edith's attention was elsewhere. And when he stooped down to pick little Kermit up, Ted would cling so tightly to one of his legs that he could hardly walk. Writing to his mother-in-law in the fall of 1890, TR exulted that he took "the utmost possible enjoyment out of my three children."

A year later there were four.

A sturdy girl, Ethel, was born the following August. The attending physician, Dr. West Roosevelt, TR's cousin and Oyster Bay neighbor, called her "the finest baby of the three physically . . . as bright as Ted but without his nervousness." She was a stocky little creature, with a build like her father's. Her legs looked "like bedposts." TR dubbed her "Elephant Johnny" and described her fondly as "a jolly naughty whacky baby too attractive for anything, and thoroughly able to hold her own in the world." Her mother said she was "the merriest baby you can imagine and so fat she waddles when she tries to run." As Ethel grew older, Edith admitted that she was "so strong and rough that I am almost afraid when she comes near me." At three she ate a toadstool and swallowed a bottle of nitrate and was none the worse for wear.

She was an incorrigible manager and ordered Ted and Kermit about constantly. When Archie was born two and a half years later, they both begged Margaret, Mame's helper, to take back Ethel and give them Archie instead. In the "gregarious nursery" (Edith's words), Ethel was quite capable of fighting for attention, particularly against Kermit. If Kermit attempted to sit on his mother's lap, as he often did, Ethel would try to pull him off, and when Edith scolded her, she would burst into tears and ask her mother for her handkerchief.

When Kermit was five and Ethel three and a half, he discovered he had a secret weapon. He had developed water on the knee and was wearing a cumbersome metal brace, which, far from holding him back, gave him an unsuspected edge. TR described the "furious war" his number three and his number four children waged on each other.

The other day Ethel took away his go-cart, whereupon he charged her like a small heavy dragoon, bowled her over, and trundled off the cart. Ethel, who possesses much determination, and the temper and physique of a miniature James Corbett, made a rapid flank movement round by the piazza, and in turn charged him and upset him. They then had it out, and she bit him and he used the weapon with which art had provided him by standing on his head and thumping her with his steel leg; about which period of the engagement a fond parent appeared on the scene and punished both combatants impartially.

Two years later, all had changed. Kermit and Ethel together had committed some misdeed for which TR was reproving them. The two little creatures were standing before him as he talked to them very sternly. Impulsively, he reached down and shook Kermit by the shoulder. Poor little Ethel, her mother remembered, her face streaming with tears, touched his arm and said, "Shake *me* father." She could not stand seeing Kermit punished.

When Archibald Bulloch Roosevelt made his entry into the household in 1894, Ethel begged her father to "hand her that little Archibald baby." Edith was understandably reluctant. Ethel was so violent in her demonstrations of affection that she trembled for the life and limb of "the longclothes boy," as Ethel called him. The evening of the birth TR had gone upstairs to tell Mame of the baby's arrival and heard Ted asking the nurse delightedly, "And have I got a little new brother?" Ted then woke Alice and they both sat on Mame's bed "chatterring like parroqueets and hugging two large darkey ragdollies which they always took to bed." When their father let them tiptoe down to make the acquaintance of their new sibling, he wrote in Edith's journal that they were as "cunning about him as possible" and proclaimed that this was "better than Christmas."

By now even TR began to think that "this particular branch of the Roosevelt family is getting to be numerous enough." That had also been the thought of a number of their friends, who had watched Edith struggling to make do with her large household and limited budget, but Theodore had always been a vociferous champion of large families. He firmly believed that among all the evils in America the worst was the diminishing birthrate among the old, established American stock. Once, when Alice heard of an Italian cabbie who had twenty children during twenty-five years of marriage, she was quick to exclaim, "How father would love that man!" So it was only a matter of time before Father's enthusiasm about his own expanding brood returned in full force.

Watching Theodore's wholehearted and boyish involvement with his youngsters, Edith began to refer to him as "her oldest and rather worst child." As for Father, "I revel in the bunnies," he wrote to Bamie, "... they all are dear."

⁓

As the children grew older, Father encouraged them to have pets. He wanted them to realize that it was "inconceivably base" to be cruel to the weak, and this was a lesson he felt his children could learn from the vast array of four-footed creatures that began to fill up every corner of the old barn and rambling house.

For starters, they had first one pony and then two. General Grant sedately drew the pony cart with elderly Mame holding the reins, until his legs began to go and he lay down too often and too unexpectedly in the road. The children all loved pony Grant, even when Ted, age three, while hugging the pony's legs with his broad straw hat tilted on end, felt General Grant munching the brim and let out a wail of anguish, evidently thinking the pony had decided to treat him like a radish.

General Grant was followed by Algonquin, a calico pony who became Archie's favorite but who was mounted on the family morning rides by any small Roosevelt who had not yet graduated to one of the larger horses. Algonquin was regularly transported between Sagamore and Washington both fall and summer and became a familiar sight in Oyster Bay and the capital, with one or another towhead astride him. Father felt there were no pets like horses and saw to it that all his children rode, albeit with varying skill. Their stable was oddly assorted, containing everything from antiquated polo ponies to Father's favorite hunter, "a gallant, spirited old fellow" named Bleistein after the man who had given the horse to him. Mother had a mare, Yagenka, and when every rideable animal was impressed, the whole family would start off "looking much like the Cumberbach family in Caldecott's pictures." How much Father truly loved both his horses and his daily rides becomes clear in his letters to his children. He devotes a great deal of time to describing these rides, how the horses are performing, their illnesses, and above all, the enjoyment he takes from this sport. From his days in the West, he tended to ride with too long stirrups, as he himself recognized, and was not a graceful equestrian. "Not a purity rider, but a hell of a *good* rider," one of his western friends described him.

Father was also particularly fond of dogs, a feeling shared by all his children but only occasionally by Mother, who tended, as Ted noted, to agree with Robert Trinder's aunt when she declared, "This house is rotten with dogs."

One of the first, a large yellow animal of several breeds, had been christened Susan by small Kermit, "because it is a nice name" and because a white cow had also had that name—no matter that the cow and the dog were not of the same sex. Susan lived many years and was a great favorite of all the children, especially Alice, who named one of her legs Susan. The other, according to Ted's recollection, she called after any member of the family of whom she was particularly fond at the moment.

A long dynasty of dogs coexisted with the family over the years, ranging from blooded collies to what Father called "Heinz pickle" dogs of fifty-seven varieties. The most loved of all was a black, smooth-haired Manchester terrier named Jack, who belonged to Ted and who was a "house dog," the type that Mother favored, rather than an "outside dog." He was given to eating shoes and the backs of morocco-bound books and each night would nose his way under Ted's bedclothes, working his way to the foot "like a miniature earthquake."

Father often returned from his hunting trips with a surprise treat for one or another of the bunnies. He fell for a little black-and-tan terrier named Skip, which rode on his saddle during a bear hunt in Colorado, and brought it home to Sagamore, where it was instantly adopted by Archie. This gutsy little cur, long accustomed to riding on a sportsman's saddle and hopping off to join the fight when the animal was brought to bay, "changed at once into a real little-boy's dog," never letting Archie out of his sight although still hopping onto any horse that would let him. When Archie took up sailing, Skip insisted on joining him in the small dory, becoming a valued member of his crew. Little Skip was run over the day before Archie was to leave for boarding school.

As Father had established a pet cemetery in a grove of flowering bushes behind the house, he would lead the solemn burial procession as each beloved dog or horse was laid to rest. So Skip joined the group, which came to include Jack, Susan, Boz, and Jessie; Little Texas, Father's horse in the Spanish-American War, and Tamara, Ted's horse in World War I. The great granite boulder marking the spot is cut with the simple inscription "Faithful Friends" and the names of each special pet listed beneath.

The children also had guinea pigs. It was the fashion at the time for small boys to wear sailor blouses gathered at the waist by elastic, and these acted as the perfect carryalls for the Roosevelt guinea pigs, who would run around the waistbands while the boys proceeded with their business. One of the guinea pigs was of unusual size and was christened by Ted the Prodigal Son. When Father wondered why in the world he had given it such a name, he discovered that Ted "regarded prodigal as a synonym of prodigious—an adjective of immensity."

Father's position in the world resulted in his being the recipient, as he wryly recalled, of "a fairly appalling number of animals, from known and unknown friends":

In one year the list included—besides a lion, a hyena, and a zebra from the Emperor of Ethiopia—five bears, a wildcat, a coyote, two macaws, an eagle, a barn owl, and several snakes and lizards. Most of these went to the Zoo but a few were kept by the children. Those thus kept numbered at one end of the scale gentle, trustful, pretty things, like kangaroo rats and flying squirrels; and at the other end a queer-tempered young black bear, which the children named Jonathan Edwards, partly because of certain well-marked Calvinistic tendencies in his disposition, partly out of compliment to their mother, whose ancestors included that Puritan divine. The kangaroo rats and flying squirrels slept in their pockets and blouses, went to school with them, and sometimes unexpectedly appeared at breakfast or dinner. The bear added zest to life in more ways than one. When we took him to walk, it was always with a chain and club; and when at last he went to the Zoo, the entire household breathed a sigh of relief, although I think the dogs missed him, as he had occasionally yielded them the pleasure of the chase in its strongest form.

In 1903, when Father was touring western Kansas, he was given a baby badger by a little girl whose brother had captured it. TR named it Josiah, after the boy, and took it home to Sagamore, where the children received it ecstatically. It was Archie, again, who became Josiah's special friend and carried him about, as his father noted, "usually tightly clasped round where his waist would have been if he had one," looking much like "a small mattress with a leg at each corner." Josiah hissed when angry and was prone to nipping legs. Archie soon learned to sit with his legs safely tucked under him but never let the badger's short-temperedness interrupt their amicable relationship.

As though these land-based creatures were not enough in one house, Father once met Archie going in to his bath and was cordially invited in to see the livestock. "There were tadpoles in a jar," he reported to Ted, "four wee turtles in the bath tub, and a small alligator in the basin. Mademoiselle [a French governess hired to improve the two youngest boys' mastery of that language and their general deportment] told me that Archie regarded the turtles 'avec beaucoup de tendresse,' but found the alligator 'antipathetique'—I hope my spelling is right!"

⌒

When Quentin arrived on the scene in November of 1897, the Roosevelt family was finally complete and came to be known as the Roosevelt half dozen. The other children took to him instantly, as did his father, and of all his sons Quentin was to be the most like him. Their stocky builds were similar, as were their agile minds.

The winter of Quentin's birth was a decisive one for TR. He had been appointed assistant secretary of the Navy in the preceding April following his two years as police commissioner of New York City. Tensions with Spain had been building over the increase of Spanish repression in the Caribbean, notably in Cuba, and TR was soon convinced that a build-up of naval power was the logical response. As the year wore on, he became a leading spokesman for the growing expansionist movement in the United States, feeling that war was definitely in the future and that when it came *"it should come finally on our initiative,* and after we have had time to prepare." At the end of January the battleship *Maine* was dispatched to Havana Harbor as "an act of friendly courtesy." On February 15 it blew up, with a loss of 262 lives, but it was not until two months later— April 19, exactly one year from the day TR had assumed his duties as assistant secretary of the Navy—that President McKinley and the Congress resolved for Cuban independence and the war was on. It was a war in which TR had already made clear he intended to fight.

TR resigned from the Navy Department on May 6, 1898, and with his friend Captain Leonard Wood set about organizing a volunteer cavalry regiment made up in part of his cowboy friends, men from eastern colleges, even a few policemen who had worked under him in New York City. The regiment was dubbed the Rough Riders; Wood became its colonel and TR its lieutenant colonel.

When the day arrived for Father to set off for Texas, where the regiment would undergo a short period of training, the four older children were, quite naturally, vastly excited and impressed as they watched him pack his trunk and tuck in twelve extra pairs of spectacles. The stress of leaving home, TR recalled, was somewhat lightened by Kermit, "whose ideas of what was about to happen were hazy, clasping me round the legs with a beaming smile and saying, 'and is my father going to the war? And will he bring back a bear?'" Later, Kermit wrote proudly to Aunt Emily, "Father went to war last Thursday. I sted up until he left which was 10. . . ."

In May Father cabled Edith in Washington that his regiment was being transferred to Tampa, Florida, prior to boarding the transports to Cuba. When Ted heard that his father was about to ship out, his mother reported, "He says he should think every boy should want to go to war and wished you could have taken him just to clean your guns for of course he would not expect a shot at the enemy! . . . Ted hopes there will be one battle so that you can be in it, but come out safe. Not every boy has a father who has seen a battle he says."

The regiment embarked for Cuba on June 13, and on June 24 the Rough Riders saw their first action. Not surprisingly, TR was a born commander. When on July 1 he was ordered to attack the San Juan highlands overlooking Santiago, he fearlessly led the charge, waving his distinctive Rough Rider hat and inspiring the men to follow him. This "crowded hour," resulting in a remarkable victory for the American forces, was perhaps the greatest moment in Father's life.

He was never far from his children's thoughts. Despite his admiration for the father at war, little Ted missed him and was full of anxiety. One evening in saying his prayers, he asked his mother to make one for him. "He said," Edith wrote TR, " 'I want to pray to have Father brought home safe from the war, but when I try I get all mixed up with the 'ye's—but perhaps thinking it is just as good.' "

In June the children and Edith were back at Sagamore. Six-year-old Ethel remembered sitting on the back steps of the porch sewing or folding bandages for the Rough Riders. "I wrote him letters, and was sorry he was away," she recalled. Edith reported to TR that Kermit had said, "It seems very strange at Sagamore without Father." He went on to ask if his father would be home soon and if he would fight any more. Edith found it "hard to answer his questions truthfully without alarming him." Even little Archie talked of his father all day long, she told TR. "His favorite play is bringing Father home on his little choochoos and he says 'I think of Father all-the-daytime.' "

Edith and the children were never far from Father's thoughts either. During one day's fighting, with snipers' bullets whizzing about him, Father was picking up spent cartridges as souvenirs for the boys. He wrote to Edith that if he was killed, she should give his sword and revolver to Ted and Kermit. But it was not in TR's nature to dwell on death and defeat. To him it was a "bully fight," and as the summer progressed Alice and Ted themselves began to enjoy the war news thoroughly, tramping up and down the piazza at Sagamore shouting warlike verses from "The Saga of King Olaf," which they had learned by heart at their father's knee.

In July Alice received a letter from her father that she kept and had framed and which now hangs on the wall of her granddaughter's house.

near Santiago
July 18th, '98

Darling Alice,

I was very glad to get your letter, and to hear of all you had done.

I have had a very hard and dangerous month. I have enjoyed it, too, in a way; but war is a grim and fearful thing. It is strange to see "Nicanor lie dead in his harness," when Nicanor and you have that morning spoken together with eager longing of glory and honor to be won or lost, and of the loved ones who will be thrilled or struck down according as the event of the day goes. Worse still is the awful agony of the field hospital where the wounded lie day and night in the mud, drenched with rain and scorched with the terrible sun; while the sky overhead is darkened by the whirling vultures and the stream of staring fugitives, the poor emaciated women

and the little tots of children, some like Archie and Quentin.
One poor little mite still carried a canary in a little cage. My
men are not well fed, and they are fierce and terrible in battle;
but they [gave] half they had to the poor women and children.
I suppose a good many of them thought, as I did, of their own
wives or sisters and little ones. War is often, as this one is,
necessary and righteous; but it is terrible.

Your loving father
T.R.

This letter to Alice was written seventeen days after TR's charge up
San Juan Hill—and into history. Overnight Theodore Roosevelt
had become the most famous man in America, a hero to his coun-
trymen and, most assuredly, to his children. TR, himself, felt ful-
filled. He confided to his brother-in-law, "It makes me feel as
though I could now leave something to my children which will
serve as an apology for my having existed." After an anxious six
weeks fighting to get his men leave from the malaria- and yellow-
fever-infested atmosphere of Cuba, the Rough Riders were finally
put on a ship for home. Their landing destination was Montauk
Point, Long Island, a mere hundred odd miles from Oyster Bay.

The children, wild with excitement at the imminent return of
their father, wanted to deck the house with bunting in celebration.
Mother would not allow it; it would not be in good taste. She finally
gave her consent for a cardboard banner, nailed to a stick, to adorn
the lawn and catch his eye. It would say: IN HONOR OF COLONEL
ROOSEVELT'S RETURN. Mother had no idea of the celebration that
would erupt when her husband came back to Oyster Bay on a four-
day pass. Bunting indeed! It was rockets and cannons and muskets,
bonfires and banners. The little village had never extended such a
glorious and affectionate outpouring for one of its own.

Rumor had spread even before TR set foot back on his native soil that he was a leading candidate for governor of the state of New York, so that Sagamore was soon crawling with reporters. One collared Archie. "Where is the Colonel?" he demanded. "I don't know where the Colonel is," replied Archie, "but Father is taking a bath."

When TR's leave was over and he returned to Camp Wyckoff at Montauk, the children pestered their mother to take them to see the Rough Riders they had heard so much about. Two weeks later, on a sparkling September day, Mother took Alice, Ted, Kermit, and Ethel on a "never-to-be-forgotten twenty-four hours," as Alice recalled their visit to TR's camp. "I was fourteen and a half years old and I felt every inch the 'Colonel's daughter,' and if I was in love with one Rough Rider, I was in love with twenty, even though I did have a pigtail and short dresses."

Ted and Kermit had a splendid time sleeping in their father's tent, one on his cot and the other on his air mattress, while TR had to make do on the table.

The Rough Riders were mustered out a short while later, a month after arriving at Long Island, and presented their beloved colonel with a gift that touched him deeply. It was Frederic Remington's statue *Bronco Buster*, the very personification of his Rough Riders. "This is something I shall hand down to my children," TR told them, his voice breaking.

⁓

TR then returned to Edith and his bunnies at Sagamore, eager to reacquaint himself with his youngest son, not yet a year old, and to decide whether making the run for governor was a good idea for him and for his family. Once settled that he would make the race, he put into it all of his tremendous energy and enthusiasm, and the year 1899 found the family happily occupying the governor's mansion in Albany.

But summers were still reserved for Sagamore as indeed they were when Father left the governorship to become vice president and then president. On rainy days there was the "gun room." When planning the use of the rooms at Sagamore, TR had written Bamie that he intended to fit up the top room as his study, the library being too central and too full of disturbances. This would be a room to which people were not to come—"not even the guests, unless I specially invite them." This rule did not apply to the children, as it turned out, and they invaded it as they pleased. Originally known as "the den," it was designated the "gun room" by Ted junior, and the name stuck because it was there that father and sons kept their arsenal, including a weapon that always spelled romance to them, their father's 30-30 Winchester with fang marks on its butt where a mountain lion had chewed it. The gun room had two closets—one improbably containing Mother's dresses and trunks in which she kept her precious things. Mother gave Ethel something from the trunks on every birthday, her daughter remembered—a pin, or a locket, or once a little blue enamel cross. The other closet ran back under the eaves like a robber's cave and was filled with cartridge boxes, leather cases, ramrods, old pistols, and all the paraphernalia that collects around a sportsman. The children spent hours in it, never knowing what treasure they might unearth rooting among its contents.

One of the children's favorite amusements was an obstacle race in the old barn when it was full of hay. Father held the stopwatch and egged on the contestants loudly but impartially. Each child would start from outside the barn door, dash inside, clamber either over or through the hay on the right, back up a beam to the hay on the left, then out the window, up or under three fences, before racing around the barn and back to the starting point. Records were kept with as much care as if they were competing in the Olympics, Ted remembered.

About a mile from the house a gigantic sandbank, fully two hundred feet high, rose from the edge of the bay. It was called Cooper's Bluff and was another famous place for family handicap races. It could be quite terrifying, and if the tide was high or you were unable to stop the impetus of your headlong descent, you ended up in the water. Father considered this possibility an "added thrill." Alice regarded it all somewhat differently. "Oh, those perfectly awful endurance tests masquerading as games!" she recalled. "They were rugged to a degree. Very good, I suppose, if one didn't cut oneself to pieces. I cut my head open once somersaulting down Cooper's Bluff . . . and had to be driven to the village by my parents in order to have my head sewn up." Little Quentin, on the other hand, was fearless. "Yesterday he not only ran down Cooper's Bluff quite alone," Edith wrote Emily, "but climbed it in the same way, much to Senator Cameron's delight. He watched him with interest, and exclaimed 'he has the blood!' when the small blue object neared the top."

In these adventures, and indeed in all the round-the-clock activities on which the six Roosevelt children embarked as they grew older and more skilled, they were joined by their cousins from the J. West and Emlen Roosevelt families, who were their closest neighbors and indeed their closest friends. The magnet that drew them all to Sagamore was, of course, their cousin Theodore, the ringleader of all their strenuous games even after he became president.

When one cousin was upbraided by her mother for getting wet on a hike and she explained that she was only following her cousin Theodore, as leader, that mother retorted: "Just because your cousin Theodore behaves like an *idiot* is no reason why *you* should behave like an idiot."

Maternal opposition served only to enhance cousin Theodore's standing among the young, however, and resignation soon set in as the mothers came to realize that these hikes were not just spur-of-the-minute events but often the result of careful advance planning. On a June day in Washington, obviously looking forward to shedding the cares of his office and heading for Sagamore, TR wrote Kermit:

> When we get home I intend to take all the children who care to go on one new kind of scramble walk. We'll all go in as few old clothes as possible; first, through the woods across to Fleet's pond; then swim the pond in our clothes; walk across to Cold Spring Harbor, on the Swan's shore; swim diagonally (only a hundred feet or so) to Cousin Emlen's beach; then go straight across the marsh (we must choose a time of high tide); then straight to our several homes to get clean and dry.

Needless to say, before graduating to these really serious walks, all the Roosevelt children were taught to swim. Ted remembers his mother decorously clad in an enormous heavy bathing suit, complete with skirts and pantalettes that came down to her ankles, while his father wore, as he described it, a very odd garment "of which I have never seen a duplicate. It was made in one piece and buttoned down the front. There were little half-sleeves which came just below his shoulders."

However, Father was proud of his suit, and on one occasion when he and Mother were bathing with some of their friends he called on them to admire it, little realizing that the day before his sons and their cousins had been practicing with a new rifle and had selected as their target the red side of the Roosevelt bathhouse. The proudly exhibited suit was "punctured with a series of holes like the bottom of a sieve," exposing much of the presidential backside.

As a child, TR had been so at home in the water that Bamie had said he was amphibious. One of the old local fishermen used to say, as Bamie recalled, that he was sure "dem Roosevelts were web-footed," as no one ever knew when they were in or out of the water. One day, a story goes, a young girl walking on the shore on a blustery day saw a head bobbing up and down in the whitecaps. Worried, she ran up to tell a longshoreman digging clams that there was a man in danger of drowning. Turning his leathery face seaward to where she pointed, the clammer retorted, "That man in danger? Hell, no! It's Roosevelt."

Not all the Roosevelt children, however, took after their father as they were tossed off the pier into water way above their heads. Alice finally mastered these plunges, but never the art of diving off the float. "I can see my father . . . shouting to me from the water, 'Dive, Alicy, dive.' And there was I trembling on the bank saying through tears, 'Yes, Father,' to this sea monster who was flailing away in the water, peering near-sightedly at me without glasses and with his mustache glistening wet in the sunlight. It was pathetic . . . I cried. I snarled. I hated." It was a family joke that the volume of tears shed during one of Alice's diving lessons caused the tide to rise.

An occasional visitor to Sagamore over the summer vacations was shy young Eleanor Roosevelt, daughter of TR's younger brother, Elliott. She was not one of the Oyster Bay cousins, but she was Uncle Ted's favorite niece, and once when she arrived at the house, he pounced on her with such gusto that he tore all the gathers out of her frock and both buttonholes out of her petticoat, as Edith reported to Emily. Despite his affection for her, Eleanor was not spared the customary exposure to the delights of Cold Spring

Harbor. Although she could not swim a stroke, she too was in-structed to jump off the dock and, being Eleanor, meekly obeyed although overcome with terror as she went under and came up spluttering, getting in return an approving second ducking from her mentor. At that moment she vowed never again to venture out of her depth.

One of the most cherished invitations of the summer was to join TR on an overnight camping trip. These were generally taken to Sand City on Lloyd's Neck, about six miles away by rowboat. Fa-ther would carry the youngest children in his boat, while the older boys would team up in others laden with blankets and food. As soon as they arrived at their destination, each boy would pick a spot for his blanket, help make a driftwood fire, and then race for a dip in the Sound. As the afternoon waned TR would prepare supper, frying steaks and bacon for all. "Never since then have I eaten such bacon," Kermit wrote even after his many years as an ardent hunter and camper. One of Father's specialties was frying-pan bread. He would grease the bottom of the pan, then make a thin cake of dough with flour, water, and baking powder, flipping it over when it had the right consistency. He admitted, however, that he was a very poor cook, and would "only eat my own frying-pan bread from dire ne-cessity." The children, on the other hand, considered his cooking unequaled anywhere and devoured whatever he produced.

And then it was time for his ghost stories. After heaping more driftwood on the fire and draping themselves in their blankets, the children would stretch themselves out in the sand and clamor for their favorites. The smallest lay within reach of their father so that they could touch him if the story became too vivid for their nerves and they needed the reassuring feel of his clothes to bring them back to reality. However, according to Kermit, there was "a delicious dan-ger in being too near him," because in stories in which the "haunt" seized his victim, Father would illustrate the action by making a grab at the nearest child while the entire group would scream in ecstatic terror. If Father strayed from the familiar text, he would be quickly interrupted by those who knew the stories by heart and would not brook any departures from his original version. The one most loved and most often called for was "The Reed-Walker," and it has been passed down from generation to generation of Roosevelts in much the same form that Father first told it.

The tale involved two young men from the Huntington area, Gildersleeve and Conklin by name, who every fall used to row out to shoot ducks at Sand City, where there was a shooting shack for the local residents to use in the very place where the children now sat huddled around the campfire. (Father always used the names of prominent people in the area and locations familiar to the children to lend authenticity to his stories.) Now, one year Gildersleeve and Conklin were out on this deserted spit shooting ducks when a squall came up from the northwest. The sky darkened, the wind began to howl, and as the rain pelted down, Gildersleeve and Conklin rushed to the shack for protection from the elements. Suddenly, over the whine of the wind, they heard what sounded like the moan of a person meeting an untimely end. Frightened, they went to the window to see where the noise was coming from. Through the dark and the rain they made out an eerie figure, standing on a coffin, paddling down the creek toward Sand City. Transfixed with horror, they watched as the man and coffin came closer and closer AND CLOSER! "Look, oh my God, look at that!" Conklin yelled and grabbed Gildersleeve. (At this point Father would reach out and grab a child, his voice rising in excitement as he repeated, "Look, my God!") The terrifying-looking man had brought the coffin to shore, picked up a shovel and was walking toward the cabin, not through the reeds, not on the water, but on the tops of the reeds! It was the Reed-Walker *and he was coming directly toward them!*

The two young men fled from the shack in panic. Conklin made it home. But Gildersleeve did not. Years later, a coffin was found out here in Sand City, and in it was the body of Gildersleeve, *"right here where we're sitting!"*

Father's ghost stories were deemed to be the high point of every camping trip, although one young admirer, on returning from one that had lasted for four days, found that his greatest pleasure lay in the fact that "he never asked me to wash once."

One summer TR was delighted to discover a schooner that had gone aground on a point near the boys' campsite. It gave him the chance to make camping-out trips in which the girls could also be included. They were domiciled in the wreck, while the boys kept close watch over them on the shore. Father gave them the name "squaw parties," and they were immensely popular with all the "women folk."

The girls, of course, were not excluded from the more conventional sports. Ethel was often her father's partner on the tennis court, if one could dignify the area at Sagamore given over to that game by the name "court." Built in a hollow, regularly traversed by moles so that the dirt surface was extremely uneven, it was so heavily shaded that moss grew over it. If the ball hit one of the low-lying branches, it was declared a "let." Despite these drawbacks, Father was an enthusiastic player, as were the children. Walter Hinchman, Kermit's tutor one summer at Sagamore, considered TR "perhaps the worst player in North America with the exception of Kermit, who used too heavy a racquet and frequently threw himself to the ground when he missed the ball. The president, with his tumbler-bottom spectacles, insisted on playing at the net and, no matter how gently the ball was returned, he usually missed it, sometimes by several feet." In addition to his bad eyesight, Father had, in Ted's opinion, a method of playing that was "original, to say the least. He gripped the racquet half-way up the handle with his index finger pointed along the back. When he served he did not throw the ball into the air, but held it in his left hand and hit it from between his fingers."

≈

The Fourth of July had always been the children's own day during Father's ever more challenging career. But in 1900, the year he became the vice-presidential candidate of the Republican party, in addition to the campaign responsibilities accruing to that position, he had committed himself to a Rough Rider reunion in Oklahoma City on that sacred day. There had been great distress when he apprised the children of this conflict, and nothing but his assurance that he would celebrate with them later that week had satisfied them.

On his way home from Oklahoma he decided to stop off at Canton, Ohio, to see President McKinley and, unfortunately, was invited to spend the night. Although Father was well aware that, by tradition, one never refuses a presidential invitation, in this case he told the president that he simply could not accept. He had promised his children he would be home, and such promises could not be broken even for the president of the United States.

When TR finally arrived at Sagamore, he found that his children had also kept their promise to him and not one firecracker had been set off despite their stockpiling of enough gunpowder in the home "to blow it into the Bay." Rockets, pinwheels, and Roman candles lit up the sky for hours with Father supervising until all of the satiated children went to bed intact.

Father fixed up a rifle range at Sagamore, which he encouraged all the children to use. When Ted was nine, he was given his first rifle, a Flaubert. "Father brought it out with him from town one day . . ." Ted recalled. "At once, I made for his room where I found him just preparing for his bath. The rifle was standing in a corner. Of course, I fell on it with delight. He was as much excited as I was. I wanted to see it fired to make sure it was a real rifle. That presented a difficulty. It would be too dark to shoot after supper and Father was not dressed to go out at the moment. He took it, slipped a cartridge into the chamber and, making me promise not to tell Mother, fired it into the ceiling. The report was slight, the smoke hardly noticeable, and the hole made in the ceiling so small that our sin was not detected."

Armed with their .22 rifles, Ted and later Kermit practiced marksmanship with their father and were soon roaming the Neck, hunting for squirrel or possum. One by one, the boys became expert and knowledgeable hunters, able to outshoot their very nearsighted father. This in no way deterred TR. Once when asked if he was a good shot, he tossed back the reply, "No, but I shoot often."

Father was always ready and eager to join the boys on their outings, no matter how pressing the affairs of state that beset him. On one particular afternoon during his presidency, when he was engaged with a distinguished gentleman on the subject of Cuban reciprocity, there was a knock on the library door and a small voice announced that it was after four.

"By Jove," Father responded, "so it is! Why didn't you call me sooner? One of you boys get my rifle." Apologizing to his visitor, the president asked him to excuse him. "We'll finish this talk some other time. I promised the boys I'd go shooting with them at four o'clock, and I never keep boys waiting. It's a hard trial for a boy to wait." With that he bounded out the door.

The spoils of Father's many hunting trips had been displayed throughout the rooms of Sagamore from the very outset, somewhat held in check by Edith, who was not overly enthusiastic at the sight of so many furry heads and skins. In 1905 the first big change was made in the house at Oyster Bay. A large room—called the North Room—was added, and into it went many of Father's most prized trophies, including the bison he had shot in Pretty Bulls, North Dakota, in 1883, and the elk he had dispatched in Two-Ocean Pass, Wyoming, in 1891. It was on the antlers of the elk that TR hung the sword and the hat he had worn with the Rough Riders in Cuba.

Father proceeded to fill the room with all the favorite memorabilia that he had received from monarchs, artists, and friends from all over the world. To the children the room spelled ROMANCE in capital letters, and the profusion of objects told them many things about their famous father. Two enormous elephant tusks framed the stairs leading into the high-ceilinged room, a gift from the emperor of Abyssinia. A smaller pair of tusks were from a wild elephant shot by Father on his African safari. The samurai swords, in cases to the right and left of the entrance, were presented to TR by the Japanese peace envoy, Count Komura, after the signing of the Treaty of Portsmouth, which signaled the end of the Russo-Japanese War and which had been successfully negotiated by TR and earned for him the Nobel Peace Prize. The leather armchair by the huge fireplace was the one used by Father in the Cabinet Room at the White House. His beloved Remington statue *Bronco Buster* had a place of honor on the mantel. Even the cribbage board on the large round table in the center of the room was an object of fascination, having been made from a walrus tusk.

The children also remembered the North Room as the place in

which they used to gather for special occasions. At one fancy dress party, Mother appeared as a demure Puritan, Father as a school-teacher in cap and gown. The annual Fourth of July parties, to which all the neighbors were invited, were held in this great room. "I always remember dancing the Virginia Reel," Ethel wrote, "with my mother and father always at the head of the line."

The broad piazza that wrapped around two sides of the house was Father's favorite spot for "the still, hot afternoons of summer" and for the evenings both before and after dinner. Alice remem-bered her father dressing in time to get downstairs a little before dinnertime and going out on the porch to see the sun set. "He would stand on the piazza and look and look; start to go in and go back for another look—to 'see the tall Fall River Steamer lights tear blazing up the Sound.'" After dinner the family would join him there, and when the lights of the boat from New York had passed out of sight behind Lloyd's Neck, "it was the rule that the younger ones should go to bed," Ted wrote. Father would sit in his favorite rocking chair listening to the familiar "ank-ank" of nuthatches coming down from the young elm at the corner of the house. "For a while father would drink his coffee in silence," Kermit recalled, "and then his rocking-chair would start creaking and he would say: 'Do you remember that night in the Sotik when the gunbearers were skinning the big lion?' or 'What a lovely camp that was under the big tree in the Lado when we were hunting the giant eland,' " re-ferring to the hunting trip he had taken with Kermit to Africa in 1909.

⁓

"At Sagamore Hill we love a great many things," TR wrote in his *Autobiography*, "birds and trees and books, and all things beautiful, and horses and rifles and children and hard work and the joy of life." This father, whose ambition it was to make Sagamore Hill "ever remain in the eyes of his children the one spot on earth which is quite different from every other," had succeeded beyond all his expectations. As one memorable summer followed another, they continued for the parents as well as the children to be "the seventh heaven of delight."

"There are many kinds of success in life worth having," TR wrote. "It is exceedingly interesting and attractive to be a successful business man, or railroad man, or farmer, or a successful lawyer or doctor; or a writer, or a President, or a ranchman, or the colonel of a fighting regiment, or to kill grizzly bears and lions. But for unflagging interest and enjoyment, a household of children, if things go reasonably well, certainly makes all other forms of success and achievement lose their importance by comparison."

Kermit, when solemnly assessing his future at age five, spoke for all the children when he announced, "I'll just be a plain man with bunnies, like Father!"

WINTERS AT THE
WHITE HOUSE

On September 14, 1901, William McKinley died of complications from an assassin's bullet, propelling vice president Theodore Roosevelt, just shy of his forty-third birthday, into the presidency of the United States.

Typically, Father was climbing the highest peak in the Adirondack Mountains when the messenger panted up the trail to deliver the most important telegram in his life. Although he became that day the youngest president in history, his political life had been a thorough preparation for this ultimate responsibility.

TR had been elected vice president only the previous November and had been inaugurated on March 4. The entire Roosevelt family had descended on Washington from Albany for those inaugural festivities.

Ted, who had entered Groton School at the beginning of the year, arrived, at his mother's orders, arrayed in his best clothes. To her horror, he had selected the "best" coat from one suit, the "best" trousers from another, and the "best" vest from a third. The garments of the younger children were almost totally obscured by the legion of McKinley and Roosevelt buttons pinned to them. Only little Quentin was absent as Father strode into the Senate chamber, resplendent in frock coat and red carnation, to be sworn in as vice president. He had told his mother that he didn't want to "hear Father pray at the Senate," and that if she insisted on his going he would not promise to keep quiet. So he had been left at Auntie Bye's house in the reliable care of Henry Pinckney, the Roosevelt's Negro family servant. After the ceremonies, Mrs. Elihu Root, wife of the eminent secretary of war, inquired of Quentin if he knew what his father was as a result of the morning. "Just Father" was the answer, greatly delighting the lady.

Alice, who at sixteen was already an astute political observer, had followed the course of her father's career with a knowing eye. She understood he had not wanted to be drafted for the vice presidency, an office that she felt had about it an "atmosphere of comic obscurity." TR had been an outstanding governor of New York, and he and all the family had greatly enjoyed their life in Albany. When Father was literally railroaded at the Republican Convention into the job, Alice sadly wrote in her diary: "Father seems to have accept [sic] ... It is too too bad. ... My poor dear father is nominated for the V.P." But in a section for memoranda at the back of the diary, Alice scribbled in her true conviction: "Father will be president come time. I can't help feeling that he will, it doesn't [sic] seem that it is coming this convention, but and God wills it, he will have it by 1904."

He had it, by God's will, considerably earlier than even Alice had predicted.

⌐⌐

The day the Roosevelt family arrived to take up residence in the White House, minus Ted back at Groton and Alice off visiting, has been described as "the wildest scramble" in the history of that venerable mansion. "The children, hearty and full of spirits, immediately proceeded to cut loose," veteran usher Irwin "Ike" Hoover recalled. They explored their new home in detail from top to bottom and found it glorious. They quickly discovered the crawl space between ceilings and floors, where no living being but rats and ferrets had been for years. They judged the long corridors of hardwood floors to be perfect for roller-skating and bikes. They found big tin trays in the pantry for sliding down the staircases, which also were considered excellent avenues for clumping up and down on their wooden stilts, at the time their favorite means of transportation. They soon realized that the circular seats in the East Room, which had elevations in the center for potted palms, provided ideal spaces, if the plants were removed, for a smallish child to crouch and pop out at a startled visitor. The outdoor fountains, they felt sure, would make splendid impromptu swimming pools.

As seven-year-old Archie and four-year-old Quentin were investigating the grounds on the first evening of this tumultuous descent on the presidential mansion, they spotted an old lamplighter in the park fronting Pennsylvania Avenue. He was, as the story was recounted by Colonel W. H. Crook, a forty-six-year veteran of the executive office, "trotting from post to post ... anxious to get all the jets alight before the prescribed minute had expired." Watching his progress, the boys sensed a new game, and as soon as the lighter had turned on all the gas jets on one side of the park, they scrambled up post after post, "agile as a pair of monkeys," and turned them all out. All went swimmingly for Archie and Quentin until a watchman, who had been studying this remarkable phenomenon in some bewilderment, finally decided to investigate. "When he ascertained that he had two youngsters in his hands, and that both were sons of the President, he thoughtfully concluded not to press charges against them."

Longtime observers of the various White House ménages agreed that the Roosevelts were the liveliest family to descend on the poor old White House in its entire history. Ira R.T. Smith, who spent fifty years in the White House mail room, recalled, "There was so much self-expression and so much personality around the place that at times it seemed likely that Congress would be forced to settle the old quarrel over building a new White House because the old one was going to be torn apart." He remembered the boys playing soldier with the tops of garbage cans for shields and wooden sticks for swords, with their favorite point of attack likely to be the shins of a busy clerk. "They were dead shots with a beanshooter," Smith recalled, "and their most frequent target was the shining bald head of one of the telegraph operators."

Hoover, who spent forty-two years serving eight administrations, recognized the extraordinary hold this young family took on the imagination of the people of the country, and that the newspapers, which often exaggerated the stories about other presidential families, had to tone down the Roosevelts for fear of being disbelieved. "A nervous person had no business around the White House in those days," Hoover declared. "He was sure to be a wreck in a very short time."

The safety of this young family, after the McKinley assassination, became a prime concern for the Secret Service, one which was shared by a worried Edith. Shortly after they settled in the White House, Ethel recalled, the Secret Service men, who became their great friends, taught the children "never to let anyone with his right hand in his pocket come near Father. . . . We were told when we were at the theatre to always look around to be sure that nobody looked suspicious, that nobody was fumbling for a gun. If we were out riding and some-body was coming along, we tried to get our horse between that per-son and my Father. And I think now of how indignant my Father would have been if he had known we knew any of these things."

Father, one can be sure, would have been outraged. Archie Butt, who got to know the head detective during his visit to Sagamore Hill, was told that even fifty detectives could not possibly keep the peripatetic president covered and that "he really gets angry at times being followed." Most of the detectives' time was spent hunting places to conceal themselves from TR. "If we did not keep out of sight we would soon lose our jobs. He only lets us come here be-cause the Madame wants us. If it was not to please her he would ship us away." To Butt the president seemed utterly devoid of fear.

Soon after the services for McKinley in Washington, Edith gave vent to her own apprehensions: "I suppose in a short time I shall adjust myself," she wrote to Emily, "but the horror of it hangs over me and I am never without fear for Theodore. The secret service men follow him everywhere. I try to comfort myself with the line of the old hymn, 'Brought safely by His hand thus far, why should we now give place to fear?' "

Fortunately Edith had very little time to spare for such worries. She found that when she moved into the Executive Mansion, offi-cially renamed the White House by TR soon after, she had inher-ited a gloomy, run-down house whose accommodations were totally inadequate for the needs of a family of eight plus servants. The entire ground floor, with the exception of one little private dining room, was given over to public rooms. The second floor, where the bedrooms and two antiquated bathrooms were located, was split by a glass partition that separated the executive offices from the living quarters. When the four younger children arrived with their full menagerie of pets, no one had enough space and it was something of a blessing to have Ted and Alice away. "Edie says it's like living over the store," Father confided to a friend. But Father and Mother lost no time in plotting to have Congress approve plans to move the offices to a new West Wing and to renovate the entire second floor to include two guest-room suites with bathrooms and give everyone a chance to breathe.

In the days just prior to the family's move to Washington, Edith became forcibly aware of the public interest in her young family. "You can't think how much anxiety pervades the country about the children's education," she informed TR. "I receive letters from schools and tutors every day." The country need not have worried. The education of their children had always been a top priority for Edith and TR, and both contributed their particular talents to fostering it.

Reading aloud to their children at the earliest possible age, sharing with them their quite different tastes in literature, inspired a love of reading in every member of the family. TR acknowledged that Edith was "better read, and her value of literary merit is better than mine. I have a tremendous admiration for her judgment. She is not only cultured but scholarly." TR's own reading habits were legendary.

Ike Hoover described the whole family as "fiends when it came to reading. . . . Never a moment was allowed to go to waste. From the oldest to the youngest they always had a book or a magazine before them. The President in particular would just devour a book, and it was no uncommon thing for him to go entirely through three or four volumes in the course of an evening. Likewise we frequently saw one of the children stretched out on the floor flat on his stomach eating a piece of candy and with his face buried deep in a book."

Father had learned the secret of holding the children's interest. He never let them be bored. If he felt they didn't like the book he was reading to them, he promptly found another that they did like. In this way they went through much of Scott and Dickens, Kipling and Conrad, Thackeray and Shakespeare. "The books are everywhere," Father wrote in his *Autobiography*, and that was just the way he wanted it to be.

As a teacher, however, he did admit to a "pedagogical failure" with Ted when he was small. One of TR's favorite books in his childhood had been *Homes Without Hands* by the popular English writer of natural history, J. G. Wood. "In accordance with what I believed was some kind of modern theory of making education interesting and not letting it become a task," TR wrote about placing this book before Ted, "I endeavoured to teach my eldest small boy one or two of the letters from the title-page. As the letter 'H' appeared in the title an unusual number of times, I selected that to begin on, my effort being to keep the small boy interested, not to let him realize that he was learning a lesson, and to convince him that he was merely having a good time. Whether it was the theory or my method of applying it that was defective I do not know, but I certainly absolutely eradicated from his brain any ability to learn what 'H' was; and long after he had learned all the other letters of the alphabet in the old-fashioned way, he proved wholly unable to remember 'H' under any circumstances."

This pedagogical failure was, fortunately, the exception, not the rule. Ethel remembered the unique help her father could offer the children. "He had such an enormous background of information and such an ability to cover a subject both succinctly and graphically, that in no time at all we had absorbed enough information to get us over any difficulties we had." Ted recalled a family discussion "on the spelling of 'chapps,' those leather trousers worn by cow punchers. After much debate we turned to the dictionary to decide the question. We found not only was Father right but, in addition, he was the sole authority given in the dictionary for the spelling."

At every stage of their development TR was intimately involved with the stimulation of his children's minds and imaginations. "American history was made vivid and thrilling to us by Father," Alice related. "He used to tell us of Daniel Boone and David Crockett, and the Alamo; of the Naval War of 1812; of Hampton Roads and the Battle of Mobile Bay, of Bull Run, and of Gettysburg. He made them sound like sagas. There were tales too of the Indian Wars, of the massacre of Custer and his men. I think what I really enjoyed was the sound of Father's voice telling it, but a good deal of history did sink in too."

Ted felt the same way. Much of his knowledge was gotten when as a little boy he walked with TR to the office he occupied as civil service commissioner. Striding over the wide, tree-shaded, half-empty streets of Washington, "we would stop and he would draw for me in the dust of the gutter the plan of some battle." For little Ted, his father's talk of history was not the dry history of dates and charters, but "the history where you yourself in your imagination could assume the role of the principal actors."

But perhaps the greatest contribution Father made to his children's education grew out of his abiding enthusiasm for poetry. Poetry was a family staple. The children used to gather in his room while he was dressing for dinner, and to entertain them Father would recite poetry. "To learn a poem he had only to read it through a few times, and he seemed never to forget it," Kermit recalled. During their African hunting trip, he remembered his father riding along through the wilderness repeating poetry to himself, and often they would repeat the poem together. "It might be parts of *The Saga of King Olaf,* or Kipling's *Rhyme of the Three Sealers,* or *Grave of a Hundred Head,* or, perhaps, *The Bell Buoy*——or again it might be something from

Swinburne or Shelley or Keats—or *The Ballad of Judas Iscariot*. He was above all fond of the poetry of the open, and I think we children got much of our love for the outdoor life, not only from actual example, but from the poetry that father taught us."

When Kermit was away at school, he sent his mother and father *The Children of the Night*, a small volume of poems that he admired by the then unknown poet Edwin Arlington Robinson. TR wrote to his son that he had taken "immense comfort out of the little volume," which gave Kermit the opening to then ask his father if he could find a job for Robinson, who was barely eking out a living with his poetry. "I hunted him up," TR confided to a publishing friend, "found he was having a very hard time, and put him in the Treasury Department. I think he will do his work all right, but I am free to say that he was put in less with a view to the good of the government service than with a view to helping American letters." To the delighted fifteen-year-old Kermit, who had inspired it all, Father wrote: "You will be pleased to know that Robinson, your poet, has been appointed and is at work in New York."

Robinson's friend Robert Frost never forgot TR's patronage of the obscure poet. "[TR] was our kind," Frost said. "He quoted poetry to me. He knew poetry. Poetry was in his mind; that means a great deal to me."

Because the family seemed constantly on the move—from Oyster Bay to Washington to New York to Albany and finally back to Washington—all the children except the two youngest changed schools a number of times. One thing, however, was a given from the start. The four sons would attend the local public schools until they reached puberty, at which time they would enter Groton School in Massachusetts. Alice and Ethel were expected to attend the private Cathedral School in Washington. Ethel did so. Alice did not.

Alice's education up to the time of the family's move to Washington had been erratic, to say the least. Each time the subject of a boarding school had been broached, she flatly refused. "I practically went on a strike," she recalled. "I said that I would not go—I said that if the family insisted, and sent me, I should do something disgraceful. Every afternoon I made a point of crying about it . . . and then suddenly one day the family yielded." One cannot blame them. Alice had a will of iron and had made much the same fuss over being confirmed, when they again had backed down and she was the only one of the six children not to be. Compromises were reached; governesses were hired; long trips to Auntie Bye's were arranged. Alice's real education was never formal. Blessed with a photographic memory exactly like her father's and what she later described as a "certain monkey-like quickness for 'catching on,' " she had begged to be "let loose" in his library. Father had agreed, but stipulated that she must learn something she had read each day and report to him what it was. "My father's library was enchanting," Alice recalled. "He had an enormous variety of books. . . . My father read all the time, so I just followed his example."

The more dutiful Ethel enrolled at the Cathedral School. There she took "a view of boarding school which is in my opinion so gloomy as to be wholly unwarranted," her father wrote Ted, "especially considering the fact that three nights a week she spends at home. She has very good and fine traits, but if she does not develop a more cheerful nature her life will not always be a happy one."

The half sisters could not have been more different. As Alice grew older, prettier, more sophisticated, she elected to spend more and more time away from the family with the glamorous sets in New York and Newport. Ethel, on the other hand, remained a devoted family member, "a perfect little housewife and mother" in Edith's absences, teaching the younger boys reading, writing, and arithmetic, even music. Like her grandfather and father before her, she taught Bible classes to the underprivileged. In many ways, Ethel reminded TR of his sister Bamie, who, as the eldest of the Roosevelt foursome, had assumed many of the maternal duties for which Mittie simply had no inclination. "I wish you could see Ethel; she is a real little Auntie Bye!" TR had written his sister when Ethel was a very young child. To TR, over the years, Ethel became the "asset child," Alice the "liability child," although such labels do not tell the whole story. To many Roosevelt historians, there was no doubt that Alice, of all the children, was Father's favorite.

Ted was already away at Groton when his father became president. Kermit, who was to join him the following year, was enrolled at Mr. Preston's School for Boys. When asked the usual opening-day question as to what his father did for a living, Kermit responded: "My father's name is Theodore Roosevelt and—well, he is 'it.' "

Archie was sent to the Force Public School on Massachusetts Avenue, joined by Quentin when he reached entrance age. This school, which was described by one of Quentin's pals as "our dingy, red-brick public school," was once visited by an English Educational Commission on a tour of inspection. Later, one of its distinguished members was asked what had impressed him most deeply, and he replied: "The children of the President of the United States sitting side by side with the children of your working men in a public school."

When a society matron asked one of the little Roosevelt boys, "How do you get along with those common boys?" TR's son did him proud. "I don't know what you mean. My Father says there are only four kinds of boys, good boys and bad boys, tall boys and short boys, and that's all the kind of boys there are."

Truer to form, however, the young Archie and Quentin were often at the center of classroom mischief. One day the teacher left the room and pandemonium broke loose. "There was a battle, where the old blackboard accessories filled the air," one of the participants recalled, "and powdered the floor with chalk-dust. At the height of the proceedings two erasers met violently against a quart bottle of ink. The floor was worse than dusty when the teacher returned.

"In answer to her question, 'Who did this?' a Roosevelt child and a little girl both rose. Each refused to scrub up the ink. The White House pupil returned home, secure in his dignity. A note, however, followed close after—and the other children made delighted guesses as to the precise wording of it. At any rate, the lad returned to the school room and scrubbed valiantly after school hours, until he had cleaned his half, while the maid from the little girl's household labored at the other."

Father became quite accustomed to writing notes, or even to appearing at the school itself if circumstances warranted. On one memorable occasion, Quentin, intending to hit a schoolmate on the back of his head with a large spitball while he was reciting, aimed poorly and caught his teacher, Miss Wallace, full in the face. He was marched off to the cloakroom, and came back "neither effectively punished nor humiliated, but obviously very angry," a classmate recalled.

The following morning the White House carriage, bearing the president of the United States, stopped at the school door, and a moment later TR appeared in the classroom flanked by a discomfited principal. While Quentin, thoroughly surprised, turned purple, Father presented Miss Wallace with a large bouquet and, as the young classmate vividly remembered, said to her: "Miss Wallace, I come to offer my apology for Quentin's rude and thoughtless behavior of yesterday. He was illustrating to me how accidents could happen, and most inadvertently, I suspect, mentioned the spitball. I understand he did not make an altogether satisfactory apology to you, if he made one at all . . . which he most certainly should have done. And so, the least I could do, I thought, would be to come myself. Of course, even now, it's not satisfactory because—as Quentin must learn—an apology, in order to be really acceptable should be immediately made."

Miss Wallace was dumbfounded by this visitation, and as TR then smiled his famous smile, "Little Walker White's big voice boomed out from the back of the room. 'Everybody stand up,' he commanded, 'for the President . . .'

"TR turned to him, said abruptly, 'One boy, at least, has his manners with him, to-day. That was very nice of you, indeed!' He bowed to Miss Wallace and, without a glance or a word to Quentin, hurried away."

Miss Virginia J. Arnold did not have Miss Wallace's good fortune in receiving a visit from the president after she had written a letter of complaint about Quentin's many sins at school, but she did get a prompt reply on his official stationery:

Washington, May 10, 1906

Dear Miss Arnold: I thank you for your note about Quentin. Don't you think it would be well to subject him to stricter discipline—that is, to punish him yourself, or send him to Mr. Murch for punishment that you are not able to give? Mrs. Roosevelt and I have no scruples whatever against corporal punishment. We will stand behind you entirely in doing whatever you decide is necessary. I do not think I ought to be called in merely for such offenses as dancing when coming into the classroom, for singing higher than the other boys, or for failure to work as he should work at his examples, or for drawing pictures instead of doing his sums. My own belief is that he is a docile child, although one that needs a firmness that borders on severity. We refused to let him take his Indian suit to school, as he said the other boys were going to do with their suits, because we told him he had not been good enough. If you find him defying your authority or committing any serious misdeed, then let me know and I will whip him; but it hardly seems wise to me to start in whipping him every day for offenses which in point of seriousness look as if they could be met by discipline in school and not by extreme measures taken at home.

Sincerely yours

[*In TR's handwriting*] If he brings play toys to school, confiscate them & keep them.

Only once, by his own admission, did TR physically punish one of his children. Quentin had left boarding school to come home without leave and had told untruths about it. "I have had to give him a severe whipping," TR confided to Archie, "—the first real whipping I have ever had to give one of my children." Singing higher than the other boys Father could tolerate; lying he could not.

One by one, TR's sons left the White House to attend Groton. Described in one contemporary newspaper as the "Most Exclusive School in America," Groton had been founded in 1884 by the Reverend Endicott Peabody, a cousin of Alice Lee, TR's first wife. Indeed, when TR was in the Dakotas in 1886 "Cotty" Peabody had even proposed that TR become a teacher at the school, and over the years TR had been a frequent visitor to the campus. In 1904 he was invited to be the speaker on Prize Day during the twentieth anniversary celebrations. "I sincerely pity you and Kermit in connection with my impending visit!" the president wrote his eldest son. Ted had already come up against the problem of being the president's son, having had a nasty scrap with another lad who had called him "the first boy in the land." When his father's friend, the journalist Jacob Riis, visited Groton, Ted said to him in deep disgust, "I wish that my father would soon be done holding office. I am sick and tired of it." Kermit faced the same problem as the "marked man," being labeled in a newspaper article "the most conspicuous student in the famous Groton school."

Archie escaped notoriety at Groton for the simple reason that he got expelled. This was not because of his grades, which were never good, but because he had dispatched a postcard to a Groton classmate when he was on a trip out West inquiring, "How's the old Christ factory?" Even Father's prominence could not save Archie from the Rector's wrath, and he finished his schooling at Andover.

If Archie was "much the least bright" of the Roosevelt boys, Quentin was their star. According to his proud father, Quentin had "electrified the people of Groton by standing high in his class, something which neither he nor any of his brothers ever did before." If Father found Quentin's high academic standing "almost paralyzing," Edith did not. She thought Quentin so like his father that her "mental jump was always from Theodore to Quentin, as if the two were one."

That the boys benefited from Groton there can be no doubt. When Quentin had graduated, TR and Edith both felt very melancholy to think that after fifteen years the time had come when there was no longer one of their boys at Groton. "My dear Cotty," TR wrote the Rector in gratitude, "my four boys have owed very, very much to you. They appreciate it. They will appreciate it more every day they live; and their mother and I appreciate it most of all."

Father's letters to his four sons during their years at school reflect his hands-on attitude of fatherhood. He wrote often, advising them how to balance their athletics with their studies, guiding them toward Harvard, showing interest in their evolving thoughts about their future careers. He urged them to enjoy their play, but "I want you to do your work first" was his constant advice.

Despite the pressure of running the country, every Sunday Father would gather up anywhere from half a dozen to fifteen or twenty children and take them to Rock Creek Park for a "scramble," just as he did at Sagamore. On many of these occasions he was joined by his old Rough Rider companion, General Leonard Wood, and his children.

"I had a small youngster then who was just about old enough to begin to count," Wood recalled. "He was about at the stage of intelligence where he could count up to five. And one day in crossing a deep place in Rock Creek, on a tree, Mr. Roosevelt fell in. This youngster toddled back to me and he said, 'Father, the father of all the children is in the river.' He thought all these children were Roosevelt's children. But the children came to him with an intuitive sense of his appreciation and love of them. He made friends with children always immediately, and they went to him."

TR and Edith made a special point of having breakfast with the children at the White House. It was a time for them to air their plans, discuss their problems, settle their disputes. As witnessed by Jacob Riis on one of his frequent visits, breakfast was ready promptly at a quarter past eight—"punctuality is the rule of the

house, as indeed it needs to be . . . and the day is begun with dignified ceremonial by Quentin, who 'scorts' the President down stairs
with a tune on the mechanical piano, to which his father is expected
to keep step as he descends." Riis also was treated to a private view-
ing of Kermit's kangaroo rat, one of his many pets, which he kept
in his pocket and which he brought forth and placed on the dining
table. Hopping daintily across the surface, now on two and then on
three legs, the rat accepted a piece of sugar held out to it by the
president. When it had made its bow, Kermit pocketed it again and
it snuggled down contentedly, ready to accompany him to school.

Poor Alice remembered the "awful part" of these family break-
fasts, "having to kiss Father. One tried to aim somewhere on his
face but his mustache usually got in the way. He never hung it out
to dry and it was invariably wet and smelling of shaving soap in the
morning. The boys got away with just a 'good morning' but Ethel
and I had to do the kissing part. She was small and docile and didn't
mind. I minded terribly . . ." The boys, however, always kissed their
father good night even after they were grown up. TR had no intention of hastening his children out of their childhood and, as Edward Wagenknecht observed in his engaging biography, was
indulgent about them taking rag dolls to bed, or, in the case of one,
sleeping with fourteen china animals.

Father also tried to reserve time in the evenings to either read or
play bear with the two little boys, just as he had done earlier with
Alice, Ted, Kermit, and Ethel. One night, prior to a diplomatic dinner and with fifteen minutes to spare, Father went into the nursery,
where, as he wrote Kermit, "the two small persons in pink tommies
instantly raced for the bed and threw themselves on it with ecstatic
conviction that a romp was going to begin. I did not have the heart
to disappoint them, and the result was that my shirt got so mussed
that I had to change it." Another evening he had a terrific pillow

fight with Archie and Quentin. Again he wrote Kermit, describing Quentin's idea to get as many pillows as possible in a heap and to lie on them apparently on the theory that he was protecting them from his father. "This enrages Archie," TR related, "who addresses him with lofty contempt as 'kid,' and adjures him to stand up manfully and 'fight the bear.' "

All the children remembered their father uttering loud grunts and growls in a very bearlike manner when he played with them, and after they had graduated from being his bunnies, he became the Big Bear to them and they the Little Bears. Once when young cousin Sheffield had come to have supper with Quentin in the White House he proposed a game of bear, whereupon, TR related, "Quentin said, 'How can we play bear without a father?' "

As if to solidify this image of Father, a wonderful new toy entranced the American public when TR was in the second year of his presidency. He had gone to the Mississippi Delta on a bear-hunting trip during which an overenthusiastic guide had subdued an exhausted elderly bear and had tied it to a tree in order that the president might be the one to dispatch it. When TR saw the creature roped and surrounded by a pack of snarling dogs, he, of course, refused to shoot it and instantly requested that the animal be put out of its misery with a hunting knife. This act came to the attention of Clifford Berryman, the distinguished cartoonist for *The Washington Post*, and prompted him to draw a caricature of TR, his back turned on a small, roped bear, hand raised to indicate he was "Drawing the Line in Mississippi," as the cartoon was entitled, and not about to shoot that small sitting target.

Almost overnight this political caricature found a huge audience and was printed and reprinted endlessly all over the country. Postcards, books, buttons, and advertisements followed, all carrying the theme of this little Roosevelt bear. It came to the attention of a

Brooklyn candy-store owner who also sold toys handmade by him or his wife, and he was inspired to make a brown plush bear with button eyes to put in his store window, labeling it "Teddy's Bear." From that modest start, the most beloved and famous toy in the country was launched. No nursery could be without one. It became the "security blanket" for literally millions of children, including, of course, the ones whose father had inspired it.

The Republicans took the symbol of the Teddy bear to their hearts, and over time it became the standard decoration for all their rallies. Even Mark Sullivan, in *Our Times*, said the Teddy bear was "more in evidence than the eagle and only less usual than the Stars and Stripes." At the dinner in the White House where all of TR's closest friends and associates gathered to bid him farewell as he prepared to leave the presidency, Teddy bears were arranged at each place. At his death, a little poem appeared called "The Teddies Weep."

> Beneath the faded Christmas tree,
> Their long lone vigil keeping,
> I heard the little Teddy Bears,
> In the stillness, softly weeping.
> We join them in their sad lament,
> Tradition's in their keeping,
> For he who meant so much to us,
> Their Patron Saint, is sleeping.

No matter how valiantly Mother and Father might try to prevent their children's exposure in public print, it was, given the attraction of this sixsome, a losing battle. Then too, not all the children objected to being the objects of a nation's adoration. Alice, for one, positively relished it. At seventeen, she cut a dazzling figure, midway between her metamorphosis from a tomboy to a debutante. Her father had appraised her as "by no means bad looking." In fact, her pictures show her to be extraordinarily attractive. Her hair, now a rich dark brown, was swept back and up in the manner of the day, and she was fond of large-brimmed, floral-bedecked hats that set off her small, classic features and the same wide-spaced, lovely eyes of her childhood. Her figure was pure Gibson girl, and her clothes, generously abetted by her grandparents' ongoing beneficence, enhanced her natural endowments. Alice drew press photographers and reporters to her not only by her looks but by the lifestyle she was beginning to savor.

At the invitation of Prince Henry of Germany, she made a sensation at the christening of the kaiser's yacht at a Philadelphia boatyard and was promptly dubbed "Princess Alice." Her choice of a bluish gray for her dresses inspired the clothing trade to produce a new shade of "Alice Blue" and Tin Pan Alley to produce a song, soon on everyone's lips, "Alice Blue Gown." She made her debut in the White House in 1902; with six hundred people in attendance, she had "men seven deep around her all the time," as her Aunt Corinne noted.

She slid down a bannister at the White House, landing in the midst of a group of astonished dignitaries. She had a red runabout in which she raced around Washington, sometimes taking a delighted Ethel with her. She and a friend drove a Panhard in record time from Newport to Boston, breaking speed limits all along the route by revving up to twenty-five miles an hour on the open road.

She smoked! When her appalled family had no luck in breaking this unwholesome habit, their only recourse was to insist she not smoke "under their roof." So, as Alice herself reported, she smoked "on the roof, up the chimney, out of doors, and in other houses." Many years later at Sagamore, Father said to her: "Alice, perhaps I ought to have been firmer with you about smoking," to which she replied, "Father darling, it would have done no good."

Her headstrong nature impressed Owen Wister, who was seeing the president concerning the protection of land at the head of the Wind River in Wyoming. He reported in some irritation that "Alice rushed in, got something, and rushed out. Just as I approached the end of my explanation, she flew in again.

" 'Alice,' said her father, 'the next time you come, I'll throw you out of the window.' "

Wister reported that a friend once asked Roosevelt, "Why don't you look after Alice more?" " 'Listen,' he said, 'I can be President of the United States—or—I can attend to Alice.' "

In Ike Hoover's opinion, "Miss Alice," as she was known throughout the household, "went in for society to the limit" and was never known to be home in the evening except for official social affairs. "It can reasonably be asserted," he maintained, "that no one within the recollection of the oldest inhabitant was ever entertained so much as she was."

"Alice has been at home very little," TR wrote to his sister Corinne in the summer of 1903, "spending most of her time in Newport and elsewhere associating with the Four Hundred—individuals with whom the other members of her family have exceedingly few affiliations."

Alice had acquired a pet snake, which she called Emily Spinach "because it was as green as spinach and as thin as my Aunt Emily." She felt that by the number of stories being told about this small creature "one would have thought that I was harboring a boa constrictor in the White House." Her father was not amused, writing her a scorching letter both about the snake and about her having been seen betting at a racetrack.

Sagamore Hill
August 28, 1904

Dear Alice,

Do you know how much talk there has been recently in the newspapers about your betting ... and courting notoriety with that unfortunate snake? I gave you permission to keep the snake because I thought you liked it as the children like their pets. But you used it in a way that seems to show that you did as a matter of fact court notoriety ... You must not get another snake or anything like it, and do try to remember that to court notoriety by bizarre actions is underbred and unladylike. You should not bet at all, and never in public. I wish you had some little sense of responsibility towards others. In your present position your example might be one for good; but at least you need not make it one for evil. The effect is unfortunate in many ways. Remember that when you do foolish things, you make it certain that worse than foolish things will be ascribed to you. To run into debt and be extravagant as to your clothes—such pointless extravagance, too—is not only foolish but wicked.

Your father
Theodore Roosevelt

But Father saw something deeper in his daughter. She made two very public trips in 1903 and 1905 as TR's personal and diplomatic emissary to Puerto Rico and the Far East, the first time a president's child had ever taken such an active role in world affairs. A recent appraisal of Alice as "Theodore Roosevelt's Private

Diplomat" by Stacy Rozek Cordery states: "Accounts which focus only on the trivial and social aspects of Alice Roosevelt's life miss the important symbolic role that her father expected of her and that she would continue to play even after her marriage."

In Puerto Rico Alice not only laid a cornerstone but also reviewed troops. Her father was delighted by her performance and the fact that she had found the visit so interesting. "You were of real service down there," he wrote after her return, "because you made those people feel that you liked them and took an interest in them, and your presence was accepted as a great compliment." *This* letter began "Darling Alice" and ended "Good-bye blessed girl. I like your letter very much indeed. Your loving father."

The 1905 trip, which took four months, included visits to Japan, the Philippines, Hong Kong, China, and Korea, testing Alice's diplomatic skills at each stop. Elsie Clews Parsons, wife of Representative Herbert Parsons and one of the delegation, described Alice's impact in her memoir of the trip: "We had a chance fully to appreciate for the first time what an attraction for the American public Alice, as everybody called her, was. To many, perhaps to most, Alice *was* the party. This was so outside, as well as inside the country, before the trip, during the trip, and after the trip." As her father's personal and diplomatic emissary, Alice was received by the Far East's most powerful rulers, winning acclamation at every stop.

Father was delighted.

When a demented man tried to enter Sagamore Hill, telling the Secret Service man who intercepted him that he had an appointment with the president, who wished him to marry Alice, Father commented: "Of course he's insane. He wants to marry Alice." But when Alice announced her intention to marry Nicholas Longworth, an older and already distinguished member of the House of

Representatives from Cincinnati, a graduate of Harvard and member of the Porcellian Club, Father was content. Aunt Corinne remembered being told about it at lunch before it was public knowledge, and as Father did not want the table servants to learn of it, he gave her the news in his own brand of French. *"Je vais avoir un fils en loi,"* he said gaily, telling Corinne how he had talked to Nick like *"un oncle Hollandais,"* his version of "Dutch uncle."

Alice has recorded how "anything to do with sex or childbirth was just not discussed" in the Roosevelt household. To the historians Elting E. Morison and John M. Blum, she gave her version of "how my father told me the facts of life." After a gala White House dinner in honor of Queen Marie of Rumania, at that time considered the most beautiful woman in the world, TR went up to his study to read and Alice followed him. To tease him, she asked: "Father, what did you think of Queen Marie?" TR's reply, "After all, Alice, I *am* a man," was, according to his daughter, "the only time he ever mentioned sex to me."

Edith was hardly more forthcoming. Just before Alice's wedding, she came to her and said, "You know, before you were born, your mother had to have a little something done in order to have you, so if you need anything, let me know." Alice took these unenlightening comments in stride.

She fought gamely to make her wedding *hers,* and not just that of the president's daughter. "Father," she said, "always wanted to be the corpse at every funeral, the bride at every wedding and the baby at every christening." Dispensing with bridesmaids and matrons of honor, Alice surrounded herself with men, and her wedding on February 17, 1906, five days after her twenty-second birthday, was assuredly the most dazzling social event the White House had ever experienced.

If Alice enjoyed the limelight, Ted hated it and was acutely sensitive of bearing the name Theodore Roosevelt, Jr. When he fell dangerously ill with pneumonia at Groton, the newspapers carried daily headlines concerning his progress. The fact that the president himself had gone to his bedside, where he remained until Ted was out of danger, simply meant more press coverage—as did news of Archie's laboriously scrawled get-well message: "I hop you are beter."

When Ted went to Harvard, things got so bad that Father shot off a letter to President Eliot telling him how concerned he was by the reported outrageous conduct of the newspapers in reference to Ted. "I care less than nothing about what they do or say about me," Father wrote, "for I am entirely competent to defend myself and I am past the stage where they can do me any material damage; but it is perfectly possible for them to create in the minds of Ted's fellow college boys an opinion about Ted which will go far toward seriously interfering with the enjoyment and the profit of his college career . . . Is there no way he can be protected?"

Ted even objected to signing his own name to a poem he wrote while in college and which was published in *Scribner's Magazine* under the pseudonym Jacob Van Vechten. In an explanatory letter to the editor, Father had written: "I am happy to say that he, like my other children, has grown to have a perfect horror of seeming to pose in the newspapers, and he is convinced that if his name were published there would be a chance for a little unpleasant notoriety, and for the assertion that he only got his poem published because he was my son."

Being both the namesake and the eldest son of such a Renaissance figure as Theodore Roosevelt had long been a problem for Ted. When as a child he had been afflicted with crippling headaches that five eminent Washington doctors were unable to diagnose, Dr. Alexander Lambert, an old friend of Father's, advised TR that Ted was facing a nervous breakdown brought on by TR pushing his son too hard. To Lambert, Father responded:

> *Dear Alec:* I shall give plain proof of great weakness of character by reading your letter to Mrs. Roosevelt, who is now well enough to feel the emotions of triumph. Hereafter I shall never press Ted either in body or mind. The fact is that the little fellow, who is peculiarly dear to me, had bidden fair to be all the things I would like to have been and wasn't, and it has been a great temptation to push him.

However, on the very same day, Father spread the blame around a little in a letter to his brother-in-law, Will Cowles: "I guess I have pushed him a little too hard, or rather that everybody has, for being a bright, amusing little fellow he is favored and petted by all kinds of people, from the Secretary of the Smithsonian to the daughters of the British Ambassador, with the result that he becomes self-conscious, and his nerves have finally given away."

Mother, looking back after thirty years had passed, wrote to her eldest son, "You fared worst, because Father tried to 'toughen' you, but happily was too busy to exert the same pressure on the others!"

Ted had become friends with the old blacksmith at Oyster Bay and had revealed to him some of the uneasiness he was experiencing as Theodore Roosevelt's namesake. As reported by the old man, Ted had said to him one day, "Don't you think it handicaps a boy to be the son of a man like my father, and especially to have the same name?" When asked what he meant, Ted had gone on, "Why, don't you know, there can never be another Theodore Roosevelt? I will always be honest and upright, and I hope some day to be a great soldier, but I will always be spoken of as Theodore Roosevelt's son."

Alice, the fond older sister, had understood Ted's problem completely and had sympathized with him. "Poor T.R., Jr.," she said to a friend. "Every time he crosses the street, someone has something to say because he doesn't do it as his father would. And if he navigates nicely, they say it was just as T.R. would have done it."

When Father lay gravely ill in a hospital during World War I, Ted's wife, Eleanor, stopped in to see him. Ted was overseas in battle. She confided to her father-in-law that Ted had always worried for fear he would not be worthy of him. TR's answer touched her so much that she wrote it down immediately afterward:

"Worthy of me? Darling, I'm so very proud of him. He has won high honor not only for his children but, like the Chinese, he has ennobled his ancestors. I walk with my head higher because of him. I have always taken satisfaction from the fact that when there was a war in 1898 I fought in it and did my best to get into this one. But my war was a bow-and-arrow affair compared to Ted's, and no one knows this better than I do."

The fact is that Father had long been plagued by the thought that his sons might suffer because of the prominent part he had played in the world. But the boys also recognized just how much effort Father had put into their upbringing to prepare them for what lay ahead. His clear and simple precepts had guided them from the start.

"There are two things," he had told them, "that I want you to make up your minds to. First, that you are going to have a good time as long as you live—I have no use for a sour-faced man—and next, that you are going to do something worthwhile, that you are going to work hard and do the things you start out to do . . . And whatever you do, don't flinch, don't foul, but hit the line hard!"

It was excellent advice, and the boys had only to look at their own father to find their role model.

After Kermit had departed for Groton, the household was reduced to Archie and Quentin, with Ethel home only on the nights she did not remain in boarding school. Father reported to their mother, during one of her absences, that Ethel "is too good for anything with the little boys," a regular little mother to Quentin, whom she always called "sweetheart." While helping Archie with his Latin, she delighted her father by telling him that Archie regarded Homer's gods as a "skinny lot," and that his sole interest was in the tunnels, and the fact that monks are buried face downward. Father felt that this last was "a thoroly Archie-like touch."

It was Archie, of all the children, who had most captivated the White House staff, and indeed the general public and the press, from the moment of the family's arrival in the capital. Towheaded, with a beguiling lisp and angelic smile, he was the one most frequently seen before Quentin's emergence from the nursery. He attached himself to the police squad detailed at the White House and was to be found every morning answering roll call with them, saluting the sergeant like one of the boys. The little Shetland pony, Algonquin, was his especial favorite, and he rode it with reckless abandon through the neighboring streets, chaps flapping and cowboy hat akimbo. When Archie fell ill with measles and whooping cough when he was nine, Quentin was old enough to arrange with a footman to smuggle Algonquin up a White House elevator and into the sickroom.

Father never seemed to mind the interruptions in his day that one or another of his offspring might impose. In fact, he could often be seen looking out the windows of his office to catch sight of the two littlest boys racing over the tennis ground or playing in the sandbox. When they were away, he missed the sound of his "small scamps" running up and down the hall and of their voices when he was dressing.

Ethel, Archie, and Quentin were ardent spectators when their father, always eager for exercise, took up the broadsword and engaged in spirited bouts with his old friend General Leonard Wood. Perched on the top of the library bookshelves in the old Cabinet Room, they urged their father on with shrieks of encouragement.

The children also delighted in watching Father engage in battles royal with the famous Mike Donovan, boxing instructor at the New York Athletic Club, who would occasionally spar with one of the boys. Or they would be given pointers by the equally distinguished district champion wrestler, Joe Grant, on the days he came to challenge the president in a two- to three-hour match.

Physical exercise was an absolute necessity for Father, and his children shared his enthusiasm, if not his prodigious energy for it. His young military aide and chief boxing partner, Daniel Tyler Moore, characterized the president as a "manufactured" rather than a natural athlete, and TR relished all sports with the possible exception of baseball, which did not seem to interest him as it did so many of his fellow Americans—especially his youngest son, Quentin.

Under the tutelage of Father's valet, James Amos, Quentin had progressed from a player who, according to his father, "catches and bats well, although scandalously deficient in the matter of base running," into the captain of the Force School Nine, which he ruled as rigidly as the president did his cabinet. Christened the Invincibles because of the number of their victories, Quentin and the boys would practice on the White House lawn. Despite his lack of interest in the sport, Father could not watch a boys' game without being a rooter, and as James Amos reported, he always wanted the batter to hit the ball. "He would stand shouting: 'Hit it! Hit it!'" Amos said. "And if the youngster did connect with the ball, the President would shout with glee."

Quentin was also a member of a group of six boys from the school known as the White House Gang. Their escapades have been preserved for posterity in a small book written by one of the charter members, Earle Looker, in whose memory the president loomed very large indeed.

One afternoon TR took a break from his official duties in order to play with the gang in the attic. The president arrived in their midst in his shirtsleeves, signaling that a fight was about to commence. He chased after the boys, growling ferociously, and as he closed in on one of them, Looker pulled the light switch, plunging the room into darkness. A loud smack was heard as the president struck a post.

"By George! By George!" TR bellowed from the center of the attic. "Lights! Lights! Turn on the lights! This is worse—worse—than anything I've heard of in darkest Africa!"

When Looker pushed back the switch, he was appalled to see the president, his hand over his face, leaning against a pillar that had a nail in it just about at the height of his eyes. It was a miracle that TR had missed it, but he announced that he was quite all right and left to bathe his face after admonishing the boys to "never, n-e-v-e-r, *never* again, turn off a light when anybody is near a post!"

The gang then descended on poor Looker to give him due punishment for his thoughtlessness by stuffing him into a nearby cedar chest. At first the mothballs simply gave off a pleasant pungent odor; but as the ordeal continued it became more and more difficult to breathe. Looker began to panic, feeling that he was suffocating, and still the gang sat tight on the chest. "Suddenly the lid opened," Looker recalled, "and TR looked down into my face. He was quick with his handkerchief, too, wiping my face, and almost as quick to say, 'He's broken out in a sweat! The moth-balls have got into his eyes, and made them water!' This he said, to explain his wiping away my tears which I thought was fine of him."

On one occasion the gang was returning from school, perched on the back-facing seat of the trolley car and making the most hideous faces they could contrive at the passersby when they happened to encounter TR in his carriage. They promptly redoubled their efforts to make the worst faces they knew how. To their great delight, Looker reported, TR "responded immediately, in kind, and as the street-car slowed down on account of traffic on the tracks ahead, TR produced some terrifying and extraordinary grimaces, which were witnessed with the utmost amazement by passengers on the car. As the car halted, for the carriage to make a left turn ahead of it, TR leaned forward and said, loudly enough to be heard the length of the car, 'Quentin Roosevelt, and you other little rascals, I think you have very nearly succeeded in making a fool of me in public—ordinarily, a rather difficult thing to accomplish. I had the idea of asking you to hop in, and ride the rest of the way with me. On second thought, I have concluded that it is entirely too dangerous for me to be seen with you.' "

Father had made it clear, when he was swept to victory in 1904, that he would not seek another term, a decision practically everyone regretted. For Father was only fifty years old, in his prime and at the height of his power. There was no one else on the political scene even remotely like him. He designated his friend William Howard Taft to be his successor, despite the fact that Taft himself did not want the job.

When Quentin had been roughhousing a little too vigorously

with Charlie Taft, one of the White House Gang, he was brought to task by his mother. Quentin responded that it was all right, as Charlie Taft would soon be in his house anyway, so what difference did it make if he tore it to pieces! But it was the same Quentin who said to his father, "There is a little hole in my stomach when I think of leaving the White House."

Alice, always the realist, admitted, "Nobody likes to leave the White House, whatever they say. We were no exception. There is a photograph of the whole family about to leave and I must say we look as if we are being expelled from the Garden of Eden."

But Father had prepared his children for the wrench to come by reassuring them how *he* was feeling. To Ted, a few days after the Republican party had nominated Taft to be his successor, he confided:

Every now and then solemn jacks come to me to tell me that our country must face the problem of "what it will do with its ex-Presidents"; and I always answer them that there will be one ex-President about whom they need not give themselves the slightest concern, for he will do for himself without any outside assistance; and I add that they need waste no sympathy on me—that I have had the best time of any man of my age in all the world, that I have enjoyed myself in the White House more than I have ever known any other President to enjoy himself, and that I am going to enjoy myself thoroly when I leave the White House, and what is more, continue just as long as I possibly can to do some kind of work that will count. *Ever your loving father*

As he and Kermit started laying their plans for the African safari to be made after the family's departure from Washington, Father's thoughts turned to Sagamore and the life that lay ahead for him and the children. "Sagamore is our own home," he had written Kermit. "It is Sagamore that we love; and while we enjoy to the full the White House, and appreciate immensely what a privilege it is to be here, we shall have no regrets when we leave."

⌒

If Father was upbeat, the country was not. The worshipful public hated the thought of losing track of a family that, in the words of one observer, "might have been created by Booth Tarkington." They need not have worried. In 1919 *Theodore Roosevelt's Letters to His Children* was published, becoming an instant best-seller. Covering the years of their childhood and adolescence, the book allowed the reader to share again in the Roosevelt family's idyllic summers at Sagamore and their lives in the limelight at the White House.

Father had made the selection, with the help of his editor and friend, Joseph Bucklin Bishop, from the large number of his letters that the children had carefully preserved. Many of them were high-lighted by his whimsical stick drawings of animals encountered on his hunting trips or the birds, flowers, and trees that were the passion of his naturalist's heart. These "picture letters" were greatly treasured by the recipients, and although Father had felt that his pictures "are only suited for beloved persons while they are still under seven years old," his children's demands forced him often to abandon this rule.

Bishop felt that the quality that distinguished these letters lay in the fact that TR wrote to his children always as equals. He pointed out that "as they advanced in life the mental level of intercourse was raised as they grew in intelligence and knowledge" and that no matter how great the pressure of public duties, "this devoted father and whole-hearted companion found time to send every week a long letter ... to each of his absent children." The dominating passion of TR's life was deep and abiding love of children, of family and home, reflected in the letters he and Bishop chose together.

Father did not live to see his letters published. He died in his sleep in the early morning hours of January 6, 1919. Only a short time before his death, he had told Bishop that he "would rather have this book published than anything that has ever been written about me."

Countless readers agreed with the verdict rendered by Baron Rosen, the Russian envoy who became Father's friend as they ironed out the treaty ending the Russo-Japanese War, that "it is impossible not to love the man who wrote those letters."

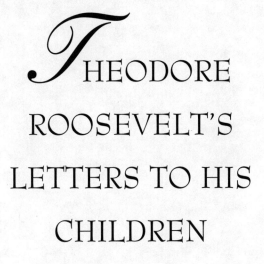

THEODORE ROOSEVELT'S LETTERS TO HIS CHILDREN

Edited by Joseph Bucklin Bishop

1919

Annotated by Joan Paterson Kerr

1995

CONTENTS

THE LETTERS

IN THE SPANISH WAR

*A*t the outbreak of the war with Spain in the spring of 1898 Theodore Roosevelt, who was then Assistant Secretary of the Navy, in association with Leonard Wood,* organized the Regiment of Rough Riders and went into camp with them at Tampa, Florida. Later he went with his regiment to Cuba.

Camp at Tampa, May 6th, '98.

BLESSED BUNNIES,

It has been a real holiday to have darling mother here. Yesterday I brought her out to the camp, and she saw it all—the men drilling, the tents in long company streets, the horses being taken to water, my little horse Texas, the colonel and the majors, and finally the mountain lion and the jolly little dog Cuba, who had several fights

---

*Major General Leonard Wood, an Army surgeon who was commissioned colonel of the Rough Riders and promoted to brigadier general the day before the battles of Santiago and San Juan Hill when TR succeeded him as colonel.

while she looked on. The mountain lion is not much more than a kitten as yet, but it is very cross and treacherous.

I was very much interested in Kermit's and Ethel's letters to-day.

We were all, horses and men, four days and four nights on the cars coming here from San Antonio, and were very tired and very dirty when we arrived. I was up almost all of each night, for it happened always to be at night when we took the horses out of the cars to feed and water them.

Mother stays at a big hotel about a mile from camp. There are nearly thirty thousand troops here now, besides the sailors from the war-ships in the bay. At night the corridors and piazzas are thronged with officers of the army and navy; the older ones fought in the great Civil War, a third of a century ago, and now they are all going to Cuba to war against the Spaniards. Most of them are in blue, but our rough-riders are in brown. Our camp is on a great flat, on sandy soil without a tree, though round about are pines and palmettos. It is very hot, indeed, but there are no mosquitoes. Marshall* is very well, and he takes care of my things and of the two horses. A general was out to inspect us when we were drilling to-day.

Off Santiago, 1898.

DARLING ETHEL:

We are near shore now and everything is in a bustle, for we may have to disembark to-night, and I do not know when I shall have another chance to write to my three blessed children, whose little notes please me so. This is only a line to tell you all how much father loves you. The Pawnee Indian drew you the picture of the lit-

---

*Marshall, TR's body servant, an ex-soldier of the Ninth (Colored) Cavalry, a "fine and faithful fellow."

tle dog, which runs everywhere round the ship, and now and then howls a little when the band plays.

Near Santiago, May 20, 1898.

DARLING ETHEL:

I loved your little letter. Here there are lots of funny little lizards that run about in the dusty roads very fast, and then stand still with their heads up. Beautiful red cardinal birds and tanagers flit about in the woods, and the flowers are lovely. But you never saw such dust. Sometimes I lie on the ground outside and sometimes in the tent. I have a mosquito net because there are so many mosquitoes.

Camp near Santiago, July 15, 1898.

DARLING ETHEL:

When it rains here—and it's very apt to rain here every day—it comes down just as if it was a torrent of water. The other night I hung up my hammock in my tent and in the middle of the night there was a terrific storm, and my tent and hammock came down with a run. The water was running over the ground in a sheet, and the mud was knee-deep; so I was a drenched and muddy object when I got to a neighboring tent, where I was given a blanket, in which I rolled up and went to sleep.

There is a funny little lizard that comes into my tent and is quite tame now; he jumps about like a little frog and puffs his throat out. There are ground-doves no bigger than big sparrows, and cuckoos almost as large as crows.

YOUTHFUL BIBLE COMMENTATORS
(To Miss Emily T. Carow)*

Oyster Bay, Dec. 8, 1900.
The other day I listened to a most amusing dialogue at the Bible lesson between Kermit and Ethel. The subject was Joseph, and just before reading it they had been reading Quentin's book containing the adventures of the Gollywogs. Joseph's conduct in repeating his dream to his brothers, whom it was certain to irritate, had struck both of the children unfavorably, as conflicting both with the laws of common-sense and with the advice given them by their parents as to the proper method of dealing with their own brothers and sisters. Kermit said: "Well, I think that was very foolish of Joseph." Ethel chimed in with "So do I, very foolish, and I do not understand how he could have done it." Then, after a pause, Kermit added thoughtfully by way of explanation: "Well, I guess he was

*Emily Tyler Carow, Aunt Emily, Edith Roosevelt's sister who lived most of her life on the Italian Riviera.

simple, like Jane in the Gollywogs": and Ethel nodded gravely in confirmation.

It is very cunning to see Kermit and Archie go to the Cove school* together. They also come down and chop with me, Archie being armed with a hatchet blunt enough to be suitable for his six years. He is a most industrious small chopper, and the other day gnawed down, or as the children call it, "beavered" down, a misshapen tulip tree, which was about fifty feet high.

FINE NAMES FOR GUINEA PIGS
(To E. S. Martin)†

Oyster Bay, Nov. 22, 1900.

Mrs. Roosevelt and I were more touched than I can well say at your sending us your book with its characteristic insertion and above all with the little extract from your boy's note about Ted. In what Form is your boy? As you have laid yourself open, I shall tell you that Ted sings in the choir and is captain of his dormitory football team. He was awfully homesick at first, but now he has won his place in his own little world and he is all right. In his last letter to his mother in response to a question about his clothes he answered that they were in good condition, excepting "that one pair of pants was split up the middle and one jacket had lost a sleeve in a scuffle, and in another pair of pants he had sat down in a jam pie at a cellar spread." We have both missed him greatly in spite of the fact that we have five remaining. Did I ever tell you about my second small boy's names for

---

*Cove School, the local public school in Oyster Bay attended by the Roosevelt children.
†Edward Sandford Martin, philosophic writer for *Harper's Weekly* and founder in 1883 of *Life*.

his Guinea pigs? They included Bishop Doane; Dr. Johnson, my Dutch Reformed pastor; Father G. Grady, the local priest with whom the children had scraped a speaking acquaintance; Fighting Bob Evans, and Admiral Dewey. Some of my Republican supporters in West Virginia have just sent me a small bear which the children of their own accord christened Jonathan Edwards, partly out of compliment to their mother's ancestor, and partly because they thought they detected Calvinistic traits in the bear's character.

A COUGAR AND LYNX HUNT

Keystone Ranch, Colo., Jan. 14th, 1901.

BLESSED TED,

From the railroad we drove fifty miles to the little frontier town of Meeker. There we were met by the hunter Goff,* a fine, quiet, hardy fellow, who knows his business thoroughly. Next morning we started on horseback, while our luggage went by wagon to Goff's ranch. We started soon after sunrise, and made our way, hunting as we went, across the high, exceedingly rugged hills, until sunset. We were hunting cougar and lynx or, as they are called out here, "lion" and "cat." The first cat we put up gave the dogs a two hours' chase, and got away among some high cliffs. In the afternoon we put up another, and had a very good hour's run, the dogs baying until the glens rang again to the echoes, as they worked hither and thither through the ravines. We walked our ponies up and down steep, rock-strewn, and tree-clad slopes, where it did not seem possible a horse could climb, and on the level places we got one or two smart gallops. At last the lynx went up a tree. Then I

---

*John B. "Johnny" Goff, one of TR's hunting companions.

saw a really funny sight. Seven hounds had been doing the trailing, while a large brindled bloodhound and two half-breeds between collie and bull stayed behind Goff, running so close to his horse's heels that they continually bumped into them, which he accepted with philosophic composure. Then the dogs proceeded literally to *climb the tree*, which was a many-forked pinon; one of the half-breeds, named Tony, got up certainly sixteen feet, until the lynx, which looked like a huge and exceedingly malevolent pussy-cat, made vicious dabs at him. I shot the lynx low, so as not to hurt his skin.

Yesterday we were in the saddle for ten hours. The dogs ran one lynx down and killed it among the rocks after a vigorous scuffle. It was in a hole and only two of them could get at it.

This morning, soon after starting out, we struck the cold trail of a mountain lion. The hounds puzzled about for nearly two hours, going up and down the great gorges, until we sometimes absolutely lost even the sound of the baying. Then they struck the fresh trail, where the cougar had killed a deer over night. In half an hour a clamorous yelling told us they had overtaken the quarry; for we had been riding up the slopes and along the crests, wherever it was possible for the horses to get footing. As we plunged and scrambled down towards the noise, one of my companions, Phil Stewart,* stopped us while he took a kodak of a rabbit which sat unconcernedly right beside our path. Soon we saw the lion in a treetop, with two of the dogs so high up among the branches that he was striking at them. He was more afraid of us than of the dogs, and as soon as he saw us he took a great flying leap and was off, the pack close behind. In a few hundred yards they had him up another tree. Here I could have shot him (Tony climbed almost up to him, and then fell twenty feet

*Philip Bathell Stewart, Colorado mining man and Republican supporter, who accompanied TR on several hunting trips.

out of the tree), but waited for Stewart to get a photo; and he jumped again. This time, after a couple of hundred yards, the dogs caught him, and a great fight followed. They could have killed him by themselves, but he bit or clawed four of them, and for fear he might kill one I ran in and stabbed him behind the shoulder, thrusting the knife you loaned me right into his heart. I have always wished to kill a cougar as I did this one, with dogs and the knife.

DOGS THAT CLIMB TREES

Keystone Ranch, Jan. 18, 1901.

DARLING LITTLE ETHEL:

I have had great fun. Most of the trip neither you nor Mother nor Sister would enjoy; but you would all of you be immensely amused with the dogs. There are eleven all told, but really only eight do very much hunting. These eight are all scarred with the wounds they have received this very week in battling with the cougars and lynxes, and they are always threatening to fight one another; but they are as affectionate toward men (and especially toward me, as I pet them) as our own home dogs. At this moment a large hound and a small half-breed bull-dog, both of whom were quite badly wounded this morning by a cougar, are shoving their noses into my lap to be petted, and humming defiance to one another. They are on excellent terms with the ranch cat and kittens. The three chief fighting dogs, who do not follow the trail, are the most affectionate of all, and, moreover, they climb trees! Yesterday we got a big lynx in the top of a pinon tree—a low, spreading kind of pine—about thirty feet tall. Turk, the bloodhound, followed him up, and after much sprawling actually got to the very top, within a couple of feet of him. Then, when the lynx was shot out of the tree, Turk, after a short scramble, took a header down through the branches, landing with a bounce on his back. Tony, one of the half-breed bull-dogs, takes such headers on an average at least once for every animal we put up a tree. We have nice little horses which climb the most extraordinary places you can imagine. Get Mother to show you some of Gustave Doré's trees; the trees on these mountains look just like them.

THE PIG NAMED MAUDE

Keystone Ranch, Jan. 29, 1901.

Darling little Ethel:

You would be much amused with the animals round the ranch. The most thoroughly independent and self-possessed of them is a large white pig which we have christened Maude. She goes everywhere at her own will; she picks up scraps from the dogs, who bay dismally at her, but know they have no right to kill her; and then she eats the green alfalfa hay from the two milch cows who live in the big corral with the horses. One of the dogs has just had a litter of puppies; you would love them, with their little wrinkled noses and squeaky voices.

ADVICE AND NEWS

Oyster Bay, May 7th, 1901.

Blessed Ted:

It was the greatest fun seeing you, and I really had a satisfactory time with you, and came away feeling that you were doing well. I am entirely satisfied with your standing, both in your studies and in athletics. I want you to do well in your sports, and I want even more to have you do well with your books; but I do not expect you to stand first in either, if so to stand could cause you overwork and hurt your health. I always believe in going hard at everything, whether it is Latin or mathematics, boxing or football, but at the same time I want to keep the sense of proportion. It is never worth while to absolutely exhaust one's self or to take big chances unless for an adequate object. I want you to keep in training the faculties which would make you, if the need arose, able to put your last ounce of pluck and strength into a contest. But I do not want you to squander these qualities. To have you play football as well as you do, and make a good name in boxing and wrestling, and be cox of your second crew, and stand second or third in your class in the studies, is all right. I should be rather sorry to see you drop too near the middle of your class, because, as you cannot enter college until you are nineteen, and will therefore be a year later in entering life, I want you to be prepared in the best possible way, so as to make up for the delay. But I know that all you can do you will do to keep substantially the position in the class that you have so far kept, and I have entire trust in you, for you have always deserved it.

The weather has been lovely here. The cherry trees are in full bloom, the peach trees just opening, while the apples will not be out for ten days. The May flowers and bloodroot have gone, the anemonies and bellwort have come and the violets are coming. All the birds are here, pretty much, and the warblers troop through the woods.

To my delight, yesterday Kermit, when I tried him on Diamond, did excellently. He has evidently turned the corner in his riding, and was just as much at home as possible, although he was on my saddle with his feet thrust in the leathers above the stirrup. Poor mother has had a hard time with Yagenka, for she rubbed her back, and as she sadly needs exercise and I could not have a saddle put upon her, I took her out bareback yesterday. Her gaits are so easy that it is really more comfortable to ride her without a saddle than to ride Texas with one, and I gave her three miles sharp cantering and trotting.

Dewey Jr. is a very cunning white guinea pig. I wish you could see Kermit taking out Dewey Sr. and Bob Evans to spend the day on the grass. Archie is the sweetest little fellow imaginable. He is always thinking of you. He has now struck up a great friendship with Nicholas,* rather to Mame's [the nurse's]† regret, as Mama would like to keep him purely for Quentin. The last-named small boisterous person was in fearful disgrace this morning, having flung a block at his mother's head. It was done in sheer playfulness, but of course could not be passed over lightly, and after the enormity of the crime had been brought fully home to him, he fled with howls of anguish to me and lay in an abandon of yellow-headed grief in my arms. Ethel is earning money for the purchase of the Art Magazine by industriously hoeing up the weeds in the walk. Alice is going to ride Yagenka bareback this afternoon, while I try to teach Ethel on Diamond, after Kermit has had his ride.

Yesterday at dinner we were talking of how badly poor Mrs. Blank‡ looked, and Kermit suddenly observed in an aside to Ethel, entirely unconscious that we were listening: "Oh, Effel, I'll tell you what Mrs. Blank looks like: Like Davis§ hen dat

*Nicholas Roosevelt, son of TR's cousin Dr. J. West Roosevelt.

†Mary "Mame" Ledwith, Edith's childhood nurse and later nurse to all the Roosevelt children.

‡Mrs. Ida S. McKinley, epileptic widow of President William McKinley, whose name was deleted from this letter probably to spare her feelings.

§Owen "Pop" Davis, the Roosevelts' much-loved Negro gardener.

died—you know, de one dat couldn't hop up on de perch." Naturally, this is purely a private anecdote.

ARCHIE AND QUENTIN

Oyster Bay, May 7, 1901.

BLESSED TED:

Recently I have gone in to play with Archie and Quentin after they have gone to bed, and they have grown to expect me, jumping up, very soft and warm in their tommies, expecting me to roll them over on the bed and tickle and "grabble" in them. However, it has proved rather too exciting, and an edict has gone forth that hereafter I must play bear with them before supper, and give up the play when they have gone to bed. To-day was Archie's birthday, and Quentin resented Archie's having presents while he (Quentin) had none. With the appalling frankness of three years old, he remarked with great sincerity that "it made him miserable," and when taken to task for his lack of altruistic spirit he expressed an obviously perfunctory repentance and said: "Well, boys must lend boys things, at any rate!"

INCIDENTS OF HOME-COMING

Oyster Bay, May 31st, 1901.

BLESSED TED:

I enclose some Filipino Revolutionary postage stamps. Maybe some of the boys would like them.

Have you made up your mind whether you would like to try

shooting the third week in August or the last week in July, or would you rather wait until you come back when I can find out something more definite from Mr. Post?*

We very much wished for you while we were at the (Buffalo) Exposition. By night it was especially beautiful. Alice and I also wished that you could have been with us when we were out riding at Geneseo. Major Wadsworth[†] put me on a splendid big horse called Triton, and sister on a thoroughbred mare. They would jump anything. It was sister's first experience, but she did splendidly and rode at any fence at which I would first put Triton. I did not try anything very high, but still some of the posts and rails were about four feet high, and it was enough to test sister's seat. Of course, all we had to do was to stick on as the horses jumped perfectly and enjoyed it quite as much as we did. The first four or five fences that I went over I should be ashamed to say how far I bounced out of the saddle, but after a while I began to get into my seat again. It has been a good many years since I have jumped a fence.

Mother stopped off at Albany while sister went on to Boston, and I came on here alone Tuesday afternoon. Saint-Gaudens,[‡] the sculptor, and Dunne[§] (*Mr. Dooley*) were on the train and took lunch with us. It was great fun meeting them and I liked them both. Ker-

*Regis Henri Post, Republican assemblyman from Suffolk County, Long Island, and a hunting friend of TR's.

[†]William Austin Wadsworth, major in the Spanish-American War and owner of a large estate in Geneseo, New York, where TR often went to ride.

[‡]Augustus Saint-Gaudens, Irish-born American sculptor and creator of the 1905 inaugural medal.

[§]Finley Peter Dunne, American journalist and humorist, creator of the character Mr. Dooley.

mit met me in high feather, although I did not reach the house until ten o'clock, and he sat by me and we exchanged anecdotes while I took my supper. Ethel had put an alarm clock under her head so as to be sure and wake up, but although it went off she continued to slumber profoundly, as did Quentin. Archie waked up sufficiently to tell me that he had found another turtle just as small as the already existing treasure of the same kind. This morning Quentin and Black Jack have neither of them been willing to leave me for any length of time. Black Jack simply lies curled up in a chair, but as Quentin is most conversational, he has added an element of harassing difficulty to my effort to answer my accumulated correspondence.

Archie announced that he had seen "the Baltimore orioles catching fish!" This seemed to warrant investigation; but it turned out he meant barn swallows skimming the water.

The President not only sent "picture letters" to his own children, but an especial one to Miss Sarah Schuyler Butler, daughter of Dr. Nicholas Murray Butler, President of Columbia University, who had written to him a little note of congratulation on his first birthday in the White House.

White House, Nov. 3d, 1901.

DEAR LITTLE MISS SARAH,

I liked your birthday note *very* much; and my children say I should draw you two pictures in return.

We have a large blue macaw—Quentin calls him a pollyparrot—who lives in the greenhouse, and is very friendly, but makes queer noises. He eats bread, potatoes, and coffee grains.

The children have a very cunning pony. He is a little pet, like a dog, but he plays tricks on them when they ride him.

He bucked Ethel over his head the other day.

Your father will tell you that these are pictures of the UNPOL-ISHED STONE PERIOD.

Give my love to your mother.

Your father's friend,

THEODORE ROOSEVELT.

UNCLE REMUS AND WHITE HOUSE PETS
(To Joel Chandler Harris)*

White House, June 9, 1902.

MY DEAR MR. HARRIS:

Your letter was a great relief to Kermit, who always becomes personally interested in his favorite author, and who has been much worried by your sickness. He would be more than delighted with a copy of "Daddy Jake." Alice has it already, but Kermit eagerly wishes it.

Last night Mrs. Roosevelt and I were sitting out on the porch at the back of the White House, and were talking of you and wishing you could be sitting there with us. It is delightful at all times, but I think especially so after dark. The monument stands up distinct but not quite earthly in the night, and at this season the air is sweet with the jasmine and honeysuckle.

All of the younger children are at present absorbed in various pets, perhaps the foremost of which is a puppy of the most orthodox puppy type. Then there is Jack, the terrier, and Sailor Boy, the Chesapeake Bay dog; and Eli, the most gorgeous macaw, with a bill that I think could bite through boiler plate, who crawls all over Ted, and whom I view with dark suspicion; and Jonathan, the piebald rat, of most friendly and affectionate nature, who also crawls all over everybody; and the flying squirrel, and two kangaroo rats; not to speak of Archie's pony, Algonquin, who is the most absolute pet of them all.

Mrs. Roosevelt and I have, I think, read all your stories to the children, and some of them over and over again.

*Joel Chandler Harris, American author, creator of the Uncle Remus stories beloved by the Roosevelt family.

THE DOG "GEM"

White House, Oct. 13, 1902.

BLESSED KERMIT:

I am delighted at all the accounts I receive of how you are doing at Groton. You seem to be enjoying yourself and are getting on well. I need not tell you to do your best to cultivate ability for concentrating your thought on whatever work you are given to do—you will need it in Latin especially. Who plays opposite you at end? Do you find you can get down well under the ball to tackle the fullback? How are you tackling?

Mother is going to present Gem to Uncle Will.* She told him she did not think he was a good dog for the city; and therefore she gives him to Uncle Will to keep in the city. Uncle Will's emotion at such self-denying generosity almost overcame him. Gem is really a very nice small bow-wow, but Mother found that in this case possession was less attractive than pursuit. When she takes him out walking he carries her along as if she was a Roman chariot. She thinks that Uncle Will or Eda can anchor him. Yesterday she and Ethel held him and got burrs out of his hair. It was a lively time for all three.

---

*Rear Admiral William Sheffield Cowles, Uncle Will, career naval officer and husband of TR's sister Anna, Auntie Bye to her nieces and nephews.

PRESIDENTIAL NURSE FOR GUINEA PIGS
(To Mrs. Elizabeth Stuart Phelps Ward)*

White House, Oct. 20, 1902.

At this moment, my small daughter being out, I am acting as nurse to two wee guinea pigs, which she feels would not be safe save in the room with me—and if I can prevent it I do not intend to have wanton suffering inflicted on any creature.

THANKSGIVING IN THE WHITE HOUSE

White House, Nov. 28, 1902.

DARLING KERMIT:

Yesterday was Thanksgiving, and we all went out riding, looking as we started a good deal like the Cumberbach family.† Archie on his beloved pony, and Ethel on Yagenka went off with Mr. Proctor to the hunt. Mother rode Jocko Root, Ted a first-class cavalry horse, I rode Renown, and with us went Senator Lodge,‡ Uncle Douglas,§ Cousin John Elliott,⁋ Mr. Bob Fergie,** and

---

*Mrs. Elizabeth Stuart Phelps Ward, author of spiritual romances depicting the lives of the poor, and leader in the movement against vivisection.

†The family from a popular picture book by English author and illustrator Randolph Caldecott.

‡Senator Henry Cabot Lodge, longtime senator from Massachusetts and close friend of TR's.

§Douglas Robinson, capitalist, husband of TR's sister Corinne.

⁋John Elliott, TR's cousin on his mother's side and intimate friend.

**Robert Hector Munro Ferguson, Scotsman who served with TR in the Rough Riders, beloved family friend, and godfather both to Ethel and to Kermit's son, Kermit junior.

General Wood. We had a three hours' scamper which was really great fun.

Yesterday I met Bozie for the first time since he came to Washington, and he almost wiggled himself into a fit, he was so overjoyed at renewing acquaintance. To see Jack and Tom Quartz play together is as amusing as it can be. We have never had a more cunning kitten than Tom Quartz. I have just had to descend with severity upon Quentin because he put the unfortunate Tom into the bathtub and then turned on the water. He didn't really mean harm.

Last evening, besides our own entire family party, all the Lodges, and their connections, came to dinner. We dined in the new State Dining-room and we drank the health of you and all the rest of both families that were absent. After dinner we cleared away the table and danced. Mother looked just as pretty as a picture and I had a lovely waltz with her. Mrs. Lodge and I danced the Virginia Reel.

A WHITE HOUSE CHRISTMAS
(To Master James A. Garfield,* Washington)

White House, Dec. 26, 1902.

JIMMIKINS:

Among all the presents I got I don't think there was one I appreciated more than yours; for I was brought up to admire and respect your grandfather, and I have a very great fondness and esteem for your father. It always seems to me as if you children were being brought up the way that mine are. Yesterday Archie got among his presents a

---

*James A. Garfield, son of James R. Garfield, secretary of the interior during last two years of TR's presidency and grandson of President James A. Garfield.

small rifle from me and a pair of riding boots from his mother. He
won't be able to use the rifle until next summer, but he has gone off
very happy in the riding boots for a ride on the calico pony Algonquin, the one you rode the other day. Yesterday morning at a quarter
of seven all the children were up and dressed and began to hammer at
the door of their mother's and my room, in which their six stockings,
all bulging out with queer angles and rotundities, were hanging from
the fireplace. So their mother and I got up, shut the window, lit the
fire, taking down the stockings, of course, put on our wrappers and
prepared to admit the children. But first there was a surprise for me,
also for their good mother, for Archie had a little Christmas tree of
his own which he had rigged up with the help of one of the carpenters in a big closet; and we all had to look at the tree and each of us
got a present off of it. There was also one present each for Jack the
dog, Tom Quartz the kitten, and Algonquin the pony, whom Archie
would no more think of neglecting than I would neglect his brothers
and sisters. Then all the children came into our bed and there they
opened their stockings. Afterwards we got dressed and took breakfast, and then all went into the library, where each child had a table
set for his bigger presents. Quentin had a perfectly delightful electric
railroad, which had been rigged up for him by one of his friends, the
White House electrician, who had been very good to all the children.
Then Ted and I, with General Wood and Mr. Bob Ferguson, who
was a lieutenant in my regiment, went for a three hours' ride; and all
of us, including all the children, took lunch at the house with the children's aunt, Mrs. Captain Cowles*—Archie and Quentin having
their lunch at a little table with their cousin Sheffield.† Late in the af-

*Anna Roosevelt Cowles, Bamie or Auntie Bye, TR's older sister.
†William Sheffield Cowles, Jr., son of Uncle Will and Auntie Bye.

ternoon I played at single stick with General Wood and Mr. Ferguson. I am going to get your father to come on and try it soon. We have to try to hit as light as possible, but sometimes we hit hard, and to-day I have a bump over one eye and a swollen wrist. Then all our family and kinsfolk and Senator and Mrs. Lodge's family and kinsfolk had our Christmas dinner at the White House, and afterwards danced in the East Room, closing up with the Virginia Reel.

TOM QUARTZ AND JACK

White House, Jan. 6, 1903.

DEAR KERMIT:

We felt very melancholy after you and Ted left and the house seemed empty and lonely. But it was the greatest possible comfort to feel that you both really have enjoyed school and are both doing well there.

Tom Quartz is certainly the cunningest kitten I have ever seen. He is always playing pranks on Jack and I get very nervous lest Jack should grow too irritated. The other evening they were both in the library—Jack sleeping before the fire—Tom Quartz scampering about, an exceedingly playful little wild creature—which is about what he is. He would race across the floor, then jump upon the curtain or play with the tassel. Suddenly he spied Jack and galloped up to him. Jack, looking exceedingly sullen and shame-faced, jumped out of the way and got upon the sofa, where Tom Quartz instantly jumped upon him again. Jack suddenly shifted to the other sofa, where Tom Quartz again went after him. Then Jack started for the door, while Tom made a rapid turn under the sofa and around the table, and just as Jack reached the door leaped on his hind-quarters.

Jack bounded forward and away and the two went tandem out of the room—Jack not reappearing at all; and after about five minutes Tom Quartz stalked solemnly back.

Another evening the next Speaker of the House, Mr. Cannon,* an exceedingly solemn, elderly gentleman with chin whiskers, who certainly does not look to be of playful nature, came to call upon me. He is a great friend of mine, and we sat talking over what our policies for the session should be until about eleven o'clock; and when he went away I accompanied him to the head of the stairs. He had gone about half-way down when Tom Quartz strolled by, his tail erect and very fluffy. He spied Mr. Cannon going down the stairs, jumped to the conclusion that he was a playmate escaping, and raced after him, suddenly grasping him by the leg the way he does Archie and Quentin when they play hide and seek with him; then loosening his hold he tore downstairs ahead of Mr. Cannon, who eyed him with iron calm and not one particle of surprise.

Ethel has reluctantly gone back to boarding-school. It is just after lunch and Dulaney† is cutting my hair while I dictate this to Mr. Loeb.‡ I left Mother lying on the sofa and reading aloud to Quentin, who as usual has hung himself over the back of the sofa in what I should personally regard as an exceedingly uncomfortable attitude to listen to literature. Archie we shall not see until this evening, when he will suddenly challenge me either to a race or a bear play, and if neither invitation is accepted will then propose that I tell a pig story or else read aloud from the Norse folk tales.

---

*Joseph Gurney Cannon of Illinois, speaker of the House for most of TR's two terms as president.

†Dulaney, Negro barber at the White House.

‡William Loeb, TR's personal secretary both as governor of New York and as president.

A FAR WESTERN TRIP

In April, 1903, President Roosevelt made a trip to the Pacific Coast, visiting Yellowstone Park and the Grand Canyon of Arizona.

TAME WILD CREATURES

Yellowstone Park, Wyoming, April 16, 1903.

DARLING ETHEL:

I wish you could be here and see how tame all the wild creatures are. As I write a dozen of deer have come down to the parade grounds, right in front of the house, to get the hay; they are all looking at the bugler, who has begun to play the "retreat."

WESTERN CUSTOMS AND SCENERY

Del Monte, Cal., May 10, 1903.

DARLING ETHEL:

I have thought it very good of you to write me so much. Of course I am feeling rather fagged, and the next four days, which will include San Francisco, will be tiresome; but I am very well. This is a beautiful hotel in which we are spending Sunday, with gardens and a long seventeen-mile drive beside the beach and the rocks and among the pines and cypresses. I went on horseback. My horse was a little beauty, spirited, swift, surefooted and enduring. As is usually the case here they had a great deal of silver on the bridle and headstall, and much carving on the saddle. We had some splendid gallops. By the way, tell mother that everywhere out here, from the

Mississippi to the Pacific, I have seen most of the girls riding astride, and most of the grown-up women. I must say I think it very much better for the horses' backs. I think by the time that you are an old lady the side-saddle will almost have vanished—I am sure I hope so. I have forgotten whether you like the side-saddle or not.

It was very interesting going through New Mexico and seeing the strange old civilization of the desert, and next day the Grand Canyon of Arizona, wonderful and beautiful beyond description. I could have sat and looked at it for days. It is a tremendous chasm, a mile deep and several miles wide, the cliffs carved into battlements, amphitheatres, towers and pinnacles, and the coloring wonderful, red and yellow and gray and green. Then we went through the desert, passed across the Sierras and came into this semi-tropical country of southern California, with palms and orange groves and olive orchards and immense quantities of flowers.

TREASURES FOR THE CHILDREN

Del Monte, Cal., May 10, 1903.

BLESSED KERMIT:

The last weeks' travel I have really enjoyed. Last Sunday and to-day (Sunday) and also on Wednesday at the Grand Canyon I had long rides, and the country has been strange and beautiful. I have collected a variety of treasures, which I shall have to try to divide up equally among you children. One treasure, by the way, is a very small badger, which I named Josiah, and he is now called Josh for short. He is very cunning and I hold him in my arms and pet him. I hope he will grow up friendly—that is if the poor little fellow lives to grow up at all. Dulaney is taking excellent care of him, and we feed him on milk and potatoes.

I have enjoyed meeting an old classmate of mine at Harvard. He was heavyweight boxing champion when I was in college.

I was much interested in your seeing the wild deer. That was quite remarkable. To-day, by the way, as I rode along the beach I saw seals, cormorants, gulls and ducks, all astonishingly tame.

MORE TREASURES

Del Monte, Cal., May 10, 1903.

BLESSED ARCHIE:

I think it was very cunning for you and Quentin to write me that letter together. I wish you could have been with me to-day on Algonquin, for we had a perfectly lovely ride. Dr. Rixey* and I were on two very handsome horses, with Mexican saddles and bridles; the reins of very slender leather with silver rings. The road led through pine and cypress forests and along the beach. The surf was beating on the rocks in one place and right between two of the rocks where I really did not see how anything could swim a seal appeared and stood up on his tail half out of the foaming water and flapped his flippers, and was as much at home as anything could be. Beautiful gulls flew close to us all around, and cormorants swam along the breakers or walked along the beach.

I have a number of treasures to divide among you children when I get back. One of the treasures is Bill the Lizard. He is a little live lizard, called a horned frog, very cunning, who lives in a small box. The little badger, Josh, is very well and eats milk and

*Dr. Presley Marion Rixey, White House physician, later surgeon general of the United States.

potatoes. We took him out and gave him a run in the sand to-day. So far he seems as friendly as possible. When he feels hungry he squeals and the colored porters insist that he says "Du-la-ney, Du-la-ney," because Dulaney is very good to him and takes care of him.

A HOMESICK PRESIDENT

Del Monte, Cal., May 10, 1903.

DEAREST QUENTY-QUEE:

I loved your letter. I am very homesick for mother and for you children; but I have enjoyed this week's travel. I have been among the orange groves, where the trees have oranges growing thick upon them, and there are more flowers than you have ever seen. I have a gold top which I shall give you if mother thinks you can take care of it. Perhaps I shall give you a silver bell instead. Whenever I see a little boy being brought up by his father or mother to look at the procession as we pass by, I think of you and Archie and feel very homesick. Sometimes little boys ride in the procession on their ponies, just like Archie on Algonquin.

JOSIAH'S PASSIONATE DAY

Writing Senator Lodge on June 6, 1903, describing his return to the White House from his western trip, the President said:

Josiah, the young badger, is hailed with the wildest enthusiasm by the children, and has passed an affectionate but passionate day with us. Fortunately his temper seems proof.

LOVES AND SPORTS OF THE CHILDREN
(To Miss Emily T. Carow)

Oyster Bay, Aug. 6, 1903.

To-day is Edith's birthday, and the children have been too cunning in celebrating it. Ethel had hemstitched a little handkerchief herself, and she had taken her gift and the gifts of all the other children into her room and neatly wrapped them up in white paper and tied with ribbons. They were for the most part taken down-stairs and put at her plate at breakfast time. Then at lunch in marched Kermit and Ethel with a cake, burning forty-two candles, and each candle with a piece of paper tied to it purporting to show the animal or inanimate object from which the candle came. All the dogs and horses—Renown, Bleistein, Yagenka, Algonquin, Sailor Boy, Brier, Hector, etc., as well as Tom Quartz, the cat, the extraordinarily named hens—such as Baron Speckle and Fierce, and finally even the boats and that pomegranate which Edith gave Kermit and which has always been known as Santiago, had each his or her or its tag on a special candle.

Edith is very well this summer and looks so young and pretty. She rides with us a great deal and loves Yagenka as much as ever. We also go out rowing together, taking our lunch and a book or two with us. The children fairly worship her, as they ought to, for a more devoted mother never was known. The children themselves are as cunning and good as possible. Ted is nearly as tall as I am and as tough and wiry as you can imagine. He is a really good rider and can hold his own in walking, running, swimming, shooting, wrestling, and boxing. Kermit is as cunning as ever and has developed greatly. He and his inseparable Philip* started out for a night's

*Philip James Roosevelt, youngest son of TR's cousin W. Emlen Roosevelt.

camping in their best the other day. A driving storm came up and they had to put back, really showing both pluck, skill and judgment. They reached home, after having been out twelve hours, at nine in the evening. Archie continues devoted to Algonquin and to Nicholas. Ted's playmates are George[*] and Jack,[†] Alec Russell,[‡] who is in Princeton, and Ensign Hamner of the *Sylph*.[§] They wrestle, shoot, swim, play tennis, and go off on long expeditions in the boats. Quenty-quee has cast off the trammels of the nursery and become a most active and fearless though very good-tempered little boy. Really the children do have an ideal time out here, and it is an ideal place for them. The three sets of cousins are always together. I am rather disconcerted by the fact that they persist in regarding me as a playmate. This afternoon, for instance, was rainy, and all of them from George, Ted, Lorraine[¶] and Ethel down to Archibald, Nicholas and Quentin, with the addition of Alec Russell and Ensign Hamner, came to get me to play with them in the old barn. They plead so hard that I finally gave in, but upon my word, I hardly knew whether it was quite right for the President to be engaged in such wild romping as the next two hours saw. The barn is filled with hay, and of course meets every requirement for the most active species of hide-and-seek and the like. Quentin enjoyed the game as much as any one, and would jump down from one hay level to another fifteen feet below with complete abandon.

I took Kermit and Archie, with Philip, Oliver[**] and Nicholas out

[*]George Emlen Roosevelt, eldest son of W. Emlen Roosevelt.

[†]John Kean Roosevelt, middle son of W. Emlen Roosevelt.

[‡]Alec Russell, son of the Presbyterian minister of Oyster Bay.

[§]The *Sylph*, a small ship of the United States Navy used by TR as president.

[¶]Lorraine Roosevelt, daughter of J. West Roosevelt.

[**]Oliver Roosevelt, son of J. West Roosevelt.

for a night's camping in the two rowboats last week. They enjoyed themselves heartily, as usual, each sleeping rolled up in his blanket, and all getting up at an unearthly hour. Also, as usual, they displayed a touching and firm conviction that my cooking is unequalled. It was of a simple character, consisting of frying beefsteak first and then potatoes in bacon fat, over the camp fire; but they certainly ate in a way that showed their words were not uttered in a spirit of empty compliment.

A PRESIDENT AT PLAY
(To Miss Emily T. Carow)

Oyster Bay, Aug. 16, 1903.
Archie and Nick continue inseparable. I wish you could have seen them the other day, after one of the picnics, walking solemnly up, jointly carrying a basket, and each with a captured turtle in his disengaged hand. Archie is a most warm-hearted, loving, cunning little goose. Quentin, a merry soul, has now become entirely one of the children, and joins heartily in all their plays, including the romps in the old barn. When Ethel had her birthday, the one entertainment for which she stipulated was that I should take part in and supervise a romp in the old barn, to which all the Roosevelt children, Ensign Hamner of the *Sylph*, Bob Ferguson and Alec Russell were to come. Of course I had not the heart to refuse; but really it seems, to put it mildly, rather odd for a stout, elderly President to be bouncing over hay-ricks in a wild effort to get to goal before an active midget of a competitor, aged nine years. However, it was really great fun.

One of our recent picnics was an innovation, due to Edith. We went in carriages or on horseback to Jane's Hill, some eight miles distant. The view was lovely, and there was a delightful old farmhouse half a mile away, where we left our horses. Speck [German Ambassador Baron Speck von Sternberg] rode with Edith and me, looking more like Hans Christian Andersen's little tin soldier than ever. His papers as Ambassador had finally come, and so he had turned up at Oyster Bay, together with the Acting Secretary of State, to present them. He appeared in what was really a very striking costume, that of a hussar. As soon as the ceremony was over, I told him to put on civilized raiment, which he did, and he spent a couple of days with me. We chopped, and shot, and rode together. He was delighted with Wyoming, and, as always, was extremely nice to the children.

The other day all the children gave amusing amateur theatricals, gotten up by Lorraine and Ted. The acting was upon Laura Roosevelt's* tennis court. All the children were most cunning, especially Quentin as Cupid, in the scantiest of pink muslin tights and bodice. Ted and Lorraine, who were respectively George Washington and Cleopatra, really carried off the play. At the end all the cast joined hands in a song and dance, the final verse being devoted especially to me. I love all these children and have great fun with them, and I am touched by the way in which they feel that I am their special friend, champion and companion.

To-day all, young and old, from the three houses went with us to Service on the great battleship *Kearsarge*—for the fleet is here to be inspected by me to-morrow. It was an impressive sight, one which I think the children will not soon forget. Most of the boys afterward went to lunch with the wretched Secretary Moody† on the *Dolphin.* Ted had the younger ones very much on his mind and

---

*Laura Roosevelt, "Cousin Laura," wife of J. West Roosevelt.

†William Henry Moody, TR's secretary of the Navy, later attorney general. In 1906 TR appointed him to the Supreme Court.

when he got back said they had been altogether too much like a March Hare tea-party, as Archie, Nicholas and Oliver were not alive to the dignity of the occasion.

TO TED ON A HUNTING TRIP

Oyster Bay, Aug. 25, 1903.

DEAR TED:

We have thought of you a good deal, of course. I am glad you have my rifle with you—you scamp, does it still have "those associations" which you alleged as the reason why you would value it so much when in the near future I became unable longer to use it? I do not have very much hope of your getting a great deal of sport on this trip, and anything you do get in the way of furred or feathered game and fishing I shall count as so much extra thrown in; but I feel the trip will teach you a lot in the way of handling yourself in a wild country, as well as of managing horses and camp outfits—of dealing with frontiersmen, etc. It will therefore fit you to go on a regular camping trip next time.

I have sternly refused to allow mother to ride Wyoming, on the ground that I would not have her make a martyr of herself in the shape of riding a horse with a single-foot gait, which she so openly detests. Accordingly, I have had some long and delightful rides with her, she on Yagenka and I on Bleistein, while Ethel and Kermit have begun to ride Wyoming. Kermit was with us this morning and got along beautifully till we galloped, whereupon Wyoming made up his mind that it was a race, and Kermit, for a moment or two, found him a handful.

On Sunday, after we came back from church and bathed, I rowed mother out to the end of Lloyds Neck, near your favorite camping ground. There we took lunch and spent a couple of hours with our books, reading a little and looking out over the beautiful Sound and at the headlands and white beaches of the coast. We rowed back through a strange, shimmering sunset.

I have played a little tennis since you left. Winty Chanler* beat me two sets, but I beat him one. Alec Russell beat me a long deuce set, 10 to 8. To-day the smaller children held their championship. Nick won a long deuce set from Archie, and to my surprise Oliver and Ethel beat Kermit and Philip in two straight sets. I officiated as umpire and furnished the prizes, which were penknives.

END OF SUMMER AT OYSTER BAY

Oyster Bay, Sept. 23, 1903.

BLESSED KERMIT:

The house seems very empty without you and Ted, although I cannot conscientiously say that it is quiet—Archie and Quentin attend to that. Archie, barefooted, bareheaded, and with his usual faded blue overalls, much torn and patched, has just returned from a morning with his beloved Nick. Quentin has passed the morning in sports and pastimes with the long-suffering secret service men. Allan has been associating closely with mother and me. Yesterday Ethel went off riding with Lorraine. She rode Wyoming, who is really turning out a very good family horse. This evening I expect Grant LaFarge† and Owen Wister,‡ who are coming to

---

*Winthrop Chanler, Harvard classmate and lifelong friend of TR.

†Christopher Grant LaFarge, architect who designed the North Room at Sagamore Hill and was a longtime friend of TR.

‡Owen "Dan" Wister, author of *The Virginian,* Harvard man and close friend of TR.

spend the night. Mother is as busy as possible putting up the house, and Ethel and I insist that she now eyes us both with a purely professional gaze, and secretly wishes she could wrap us up in a neatly pinned sheet with camphor balls inside. Good-bye, blessed fellow!

"VALUABLEST" KIND OF RABBITS
(To his sister, Mrs. W. S. Cowles)

White House, Oct. 2, 1903.

Tell Sheffield that Quentin is now going to the public school. As yet he has preserved an attitude of dignified reserve concerning his feelings on the subject. He has just been presented with two white rabbits, which he brought in while we were at lunch yesterday, explaining that they were "the valuablest kind with pink eyes."

A PREACHING LETTER

White House, Oct. 2, 1903.

DEAR KERMIT:

I was very glad to get your letter. Am glad you are playing football. I should be very sorry to see either you or Ted devoting most of your attention to athletics, and I haven't got any special ambition to see you shine overmuch in athletics at college, at least (if you go there), because I think it tends to take up too much time; but I do like to feel that you are manly and able to hold your own in rough, hardy sports. I would rather have a boy of mine stand high in his studies than high in athletics, but I could a great deal rather have him show true manliness of character than show either intellectual or physical prowess; and I believe you and Ted both bid fair to develop just such character.

There! you will think this a dreadfully preaching letter! I suppose I have a natural tendency to preach just at present because I am overwhelmed with my work. I enjoy being President, and I like to do the work and have my hand on the lever. But it is very worrying and puzzling, and I have to make up my mind to accept every kind of attack and misrepresentation. It is a great comfort to me to read the life and letters of Abraham Lincoln. I am more and more impressed every day, not only with the man's wonderful power and sagacity, but with his literally endless patience, and at the same time his unflinching resolution.

PROPER PLACE FOR SPORTS

White House, Oct. 4, 1903.

DEAR TED:

In spite of the "Hurry! Hurry!" on the outside of your envelope, I did not like to act until I had consulted Mother and thought the matter over; and to be frank with you, old fellow, I am by no means sure that I am doing right now. If it were not that I feel you will be so bitterly disappointed, I would strongly advocate your acquiescing in the decision to leave you off the second squad this year. I am proud of your pluck, and I greatly admire football—though it was not a game I was ever able to play myself, my qualities resembling Kermit's rather than yours. But the very things that make it a good game make it a rough game, and there is always the chance of your being laid up. Now, I should not in the least object to your being laid up for a season if you were striving for something worth while, to get on the Groton school team, for instance, or on your class team when you entered Harvard—for of course I don't think you will have the weight to entitle you to try for the 'varsity. But I am by no means sure that it *is* worth your while to run the risk of being laid up for the sake of playing in the second squad when you are a fourth former, instead of when you are a fifth former. I do not know that the risk is balanced by the reward. However, I have told the Rector* that as you feel so strongly about it, I think that the chance of your damaging yourself in body is outweighed by the possibility of bitterness of spirit if you could not play. Understand me, I should think mighty little of you if you permitted chagrin to make you bitter on some point where it was evidently right for you to suffer the chagrin. But in this case I am uncertain, and I shall give you the benefit of the doubt. If, however, the coaches at any time come to the conclusion that you ought not to be in the second squad, why you must come off without grumbling.

I am delighted to have you play football. I believe in rough, manly sports. But I do not believe in them if they degenerate into the sole end of any one's existence. I don't want you to sacrifice standing well in your studies to any overathleticism; and I need not tell you that character counts for a great deal more than either intellect or body in winning success in life. Athletic proficiency is a mighty good servant, and like so many other good servants, a mighty bad master. Did you ever read Pliny's letter to Trajan, in which he speaks of its being advisable to keep the Greeks absorbed in athletics, because it distracted their minds from all serious pursuits, including soldiering, and prevented their ever being dangerous to the Romans? I have not a doubt that the British officers in

*The Reverend Endicott Peabody, Episcopal clergyman and the Rector of Groton School.

the Boer War had their efficiency partly reduced because they had sacrificed their legitimate duties to an inordinate and ridiculous love of sports. A man must develop his physical prowess up to a certain point; but after he has reached that point there are other things that count more. In my regiment nine-tenths of the men were better horsemen than I was, and probably two-thirds of them better shots than I was, while on the average they were certainly hardier and more enduring. Yet after I had had them a very short while they all knew, and I knew too, that nobody else could command them as I could. I am glad you should play football; I am glad that you should box; I am glad that you should ride and shoot and walk and row as well as you do. I should be very sorry if you did not do these things. But don't ever get into the frame of mind which regards these things as constituting the end to which all your energies must be devoted, or even the major portion of your energies.

Yes, I am going to speak at Groton on prize day. I felt that while I was President, and while you and Kermit were at Groton I wanted to come up there and see you, and the Rector wished me to speak, and so I am very glad to accept.

By the way, I am working hard to get Renown accustomed to automobiles. He is such a handful now when he meets them that I seriously mind encountering them when Mother is along. Of course I do not care if I am alone, or with another man, but I am uneasy all the time when I am out with Mother. Yesterday I tried Bleistein over the hurdles at Chevy Chase. The first one was new, high and stiff, and the old rascal never rose six inches, going slap through it. I took him at it again and he went over all right.

I am very busy now, facing the usual endless worry and discouragement, and trying to keep steadily in mind that I must not only be as resolute as Abraham Lincoln in seeking to achieve decent ends, but as patient, as uncomplaining, and as even-tempered in dealing, not only with knaves, but with the well-meaning foolish people, educated and uneducated, who by their unwisdom give the knaves their chance.

. . . .

CONCERNING GETTING "SMASHED"

White House, Oct. 11, 1903.

DEAR TED:

I have received letters from the Rector, from Mr. Woods,* and from Mr. Billings.† They all say that you should play on the third squad, and Mr. Woods says you are now satisfied to do so. This was my first, and as I am convinced, my real judgment in the case. If you get mashed up now in a serious way it may prevent your playing later. As I think I wrote you, I do not in the least object to your getting smashed if it is for an object that is worth while, such as playing on the Groton team or playing on your class team when you get to Harvard. But I think it a little silly to run any imminent risk of a serious smash simply to play on the second squad instead of the third.

I am judging for you as I would for myself. When I was young and rode across country I was light and tough, and if I did, as actually happened, break an arm or a rib no damage ensued and no scandal was caused. Now I am stiff and heavy, and any accident to

---

*Colonel Arthur Woods, master at Groton who became a colonel in the Army Air Corps.

†Sherrard Billings, Episcopal minister who served for many years as assistant headmaster at Groton.

me would cause immense talk, and I do not take the chance; simply because it is not worth while. On the other hand, if I should now go to war and have a brigade as I had my regiment before Santiago, I should take any chance that was necessary; because it would be worth while. In other words, I want to make the risk to a certain accident commensurate with the object gained.

THE ART OF UNCLE REMUS
(To Joel Chandler Harris)

White House, Oct. 12, 1901.

MY DEAR HARRIS:

It is worth while being President when one's small daughter receives that kind of an autograph gift. When I was younger than she is, my Aunt Annie Bulloch, of Georgia, used to tell me some of the brer rabbit stories, especially brer rabbit and the tar baby. But fond though I am of the brer rabbit stories I think I am even fonder of your other writings. I doubt if there is a more genuinely pathetic tale in all our literature than "Free Joe." Moreover I have felt that all that you write serves to bring our people closer together. I know, of course, the ordinary talk is that an artist should be judged purely by his art; but I am rather a Philistine and like to feel that the art serves a good purpose. Your art is not only an art addition to our sum of national achievement, but it has also always been an addition to the forces that tell for decency, and above all for the blotting out of sectional antagonism.

A RIDE AND A PILLOW FIGHT

White House, Oct. 19, 1903.

DEAR KERMIT:

I was much pleased at your being made captain of your eleven. I would rather have you captain of the third eleven than playing on the second.

Yesterday afternoon Ethel on Wyoming, Mother on Yagenka and I on Renown had a long ride, the only incident being meeting a large red automobile, which much shook Renown's nerves, although he behaved far better than he has hitherto been doing about automobiles. In fact, he behaved so well that I leaned over and gave him a lump of sugar when he had passed the object of terror—the old boy eagerly turning his head around to get it. It was lovely out in the country, with the trees at their very best of the fall coloring. There are no red maples here, but the Virginia creepers and some of the dogwoods give the red, and the hickories, tulip trees and beeches a brilliant yellow, sometimes almost orange.

When we got home Mother went up-stairs first and was met by Archie and Quentin, each loaded with pillows and whispering not to let me know that they were in ambush; then as I marched up to the top they assailed me with shrieks and chuckles of delight and then the pillow fight raged up and down the hall. After my bath I read them from Uncle Remus. Usually Mother reads them, but now and then, when I think she really must have a holiday from it, I read them myself.

STUDY AND PLAY

White House, Oct. 24, 1903.

DEAR TED:

I am really greatly pleased at your standing so high in your form, and I am sure that this year it is better for you to be playing where you are in football. I suppose next year you will go back to your position of end, as you would hardly be heavy enough for playing back, or to play behind the centre, against teams with big fellows. I repeat that your standing in the class gave me real pleasure. I have sympathized so much with your delight in physical prowess and have been so glad at the success you have had, that sometimes I have been afraid I have failed to emphasize sufficiently the fact that of course one must not subordinate study and work to the cultivation of such prowess. By the way, I am sorry to say that I am falling behind physically. The last two or three years I have had a tendency to rheumatism, or gout, or something of the kind, which makes me very stiff.

Renown is behaving better about automobiles and the like. I think the difference is largely in the way I handle him. He is a very good-natured and gentle horse, but timid and not over-wise, and when in a panic his great strength makes him well-nigh uncontrollable. Accordingly, he is a bad horse to try to force by anything. If possible, it is much better to give him a little time, and bring him up as gently as may be to the object of terror. When he behaves well I lean forward and give him a lump of sugar, and now the old boy eagerly puts around his head when I stretch out my hand. Bleistein I have ridden very little, because I think one of his forelegs is shaky, and I want to spare him all I can. Mother and I have had the most lovely rides imaginable.

. . . .

QUENTIN'S FIRST FALL

White House, Oct. 24, 1903.

DEAR KERMIT:

Yesterday I felt rather seedy, having a touch of Cuban fever, my only unpleasant reminiscence of the Santiago campaign. Accordingly, I spent the afternoon in the house lying on the sofa, with a bright fire burning and Mother in the rocking chair, with her knitting, beside me. I felt so glad that I was not out somewhere in the wilderness campaigning or hunting, where I would have to walk or ride all day in the rain and then lie out under a bush at night!

When Allan will come from the trainer's I do not know. Rather to my surprise, Ronald has won golden opinions and really is a very nice dog. Pinckney* loves him, and he sits up in the express wagon just as if it was what he had been born to.

Quentin is learning to ride the pony. He had one tumble, which, he remarked philosophically, did not hurt him any more than when I whacked him with a sofa cushion in one of our pillow fights. I think he will very soon be able to manage the pony by himself.

Mother has just taken the three children to spend the afternoon at Dr. Rixey's farm. I am hard at work on my message to Congress, and accordingly shall not try to go out or see any one either this afternoon or this evening. All of this work is terribly puzzling at times, but I peg away at it, and every now and then, when the dust clears away and I look around, I feel that I really have accomplished a little, at any rate.

I think you stood well in your form, taking everything into account. I feel you deserve credit for being captain of your football eleven, and yet standing as high as you do in your class.

*Henry Pinckney, Negro steward at the White House.

HOMESICK FOR SAGAMORE HILL

White House, Nov. 4, 1903.

DEAR TED:

Three cheers for Groton! It was first-class.

On election day I saw the house, and it was all so lovely that I felt fairly homesick to be back in it. The Japanese maples were still in full leaf and were turning the most beautiful shades of scarlet imaginable. The old barn, I am sorry to say, seems to be giving away at one end.

Renown now behaves very well about automobiles, and indeed about everything. He is, however, a little touched in the wind. Bleistein, in spite of being a little shaky in one foreleg, is in splendid spirits and eager for any amount of go. When you get on here for the Christmas holidays you will have to try them both, for if there is any fox hunting I am by no means sure you will find it better to take Bleistein than Renown.

Sister [Alice] is very handsome and good, having had a delightful time.

That was a funny trick which the Indians played against Harvard. Harvard did well to play such a successful uphill game in the latter part of the second half as to enable them to win out; but I do not see how she stands a chance of success against Yale this year.

JOY OVER A FOOTBALL VICTORY

White House, Nov. 4, 1903.

DEAR KERMIT:

To-night while I was preparing to dictate a message to Congress concerning the boiling caldron on the Isthmus of Panama, which has now begun to bubble over, up came one of the ushers with a telegram from you and Ted about the football match. Instantly I bolted into the next room to read it aloud to mother and sister, and we all cheered in unison when we came to the Rah! Rah! Rah! part of it. It was a great score. I wish I could have seen the game.

. . . .

VICE-MOTHER OF THE CHILDREN

White House, Nov. 15, 1903.

DEAR KERMIT:

Didn't I tell you about Hector, Brier and Sailor Boy [dogs] when I saw them on election day? They were in excellent health, lying around the door of Seaman's* house, which they had evidently adopted as their own. Sailor Boy and Brier were exceedingly affectionate; Hector kindly, but uninterested.

Mother has gone off for nine days, and as usual I am acting as vice-mother. Archie and Quentin are really too cunning for anything. Each night I spend about three-quarters of an hour reading to them. I first of all read some book like Algonquin Indian Tales, or the poetry of Scott or Macaulay. Once I read them Jim Bludso,† which perfectly enthralled them and made Quentin ask me at least a hundred questions, including one as to whether the colored boy did not find sitting on the safety valve hot. I have also been reading

*Noah Seaman, farmer at Sagamore Hill.

†"Jim Bludso of the Prairie Belle and Little Breeches," a poem by John Hay published in 1871. Hay, a diplomat and statesman, served as TR's secretary of state until his death in 1905.

them each evening from the Bible. It has been the story of Saul, David and Jonathan. They have been so interested that several times I have had to read them more than one chapter. Then each says his prayers and repeats the hymn he is learning, Quentin usually jigging solemnly up and down while he repeats it. Each finally got one hymn perfect, whereupon in accordance with previous instructions from Mother I presented each of them with a five-cent piece. Yesterday (Saturday) I took both of them and Ethel, together with the three elder Garfield boys, for a long scramble down Rock Creek. We really had great fun.

QUENTIN'S SIXTH BIRTHDAY

White House, Nov. 19, 1903.

DEAR KERMIT:

I was much pleased at your being chosen captain of the Seventh. I had not expected it. I rather suspect that you will be behind in your studies this month. If so, try to make up next month, and keep above the middle of the class if you can. I am interested in what you tell me about the Sir Galahads, and I shall want to talk to you about them when you come on.

Mother is back with Aunt Emily, who looks very well. It is so nice to have her. As for Mother, of course she makes the house feel like a home again, instead of like a temporary dwelling.

Leo is as cunning as ever. Pinckney went to see Allan yesterday and said he found him "as busy as a bee in a tar barrel," and evidently owning all the trainer's house. He is not yet quite fit to come back here.

To-day is Quentin's birthday. He has a cold, so he had his birthday cake, with the six candles, and his birthday ice-cream, in the nursery, with Ethel, Archie, Mother, Aunt Emily, myself, Mame and Georgette* as admiring guests and onlookers.

A PRESIDENT'S POOR PROTECTION

White House, Nov. 28, 1903.

DEAR KERMIT:

It was very sad at Uncle Gracie's† funeral; and yet lovely, too, in a way, for not only all his old friends had turned out, but all of the people connected with the institutions for which he had worked during so many years also came. There were a good many of the older boys and employees from the Newsboys' Lodging House and the Orthopædic Dispensary, etc. Uncle Jimmy possessed a singularly loving and affectionate nature, and I never knew any one who in doing good was more careful to do it unostentatiously. I had no idea how much he had done. Mother with her usual thoughtfulness had kept him steadily in mind while I have been Governor and President; and I now find that he appreciated her so much, her constant remembrances in having him on to visit us on different occasions. It was a lesson to me, for I should probably never have thought of it myself; and of course when one does not do what one ought to, the excuse that one erred from thoughtlessness instead of wrong purpose is of small avail.

The police arrangements at the church were exasperating to a de-

---

*Georgette, Aunt Emily Carow's French maid.

†James K. Gracie, husband of TR's Aunt Anna Bulloch and the Roosevelts' nearest neighbor at Sagamore Hill.

gree. There were fully five hundred policemen in the streets round about, just as if there was danger of an attack by a ferocious mob; and yet though they had throngs of policemen inside, too, an elderly and harmless crank actually got inside with them to present me some foolish memorial about curing the German Emperor from cancer. Inasmuch as what we needed was, not protection against a mob, but a sharp lookout for cranks, the arrangement ought by rights to have been for fifty policemen outside and two or three good detectives inside. I felt like a fool with all the policemen in solemn and purposeless lines around about; and then I felt half exasperated and half amused when I found that they were utterly helpless to prevent a crank from getting inside after all.

P.S.—I enclose two original poems by Nick and Archie. They refer to a bit of unhappy advice I gave them, because of which I fell into richly merited disgrace with Mother. Nick has been spending three days or so with Archie, and I suggested that they should explore the White House in the mirk of midnight. They did, in white sheets, and, like little jacks, barefooted. Send me back the poems.

November 28, 1903
Archie & Nick

Good morning Mr. President
Again we have to say
We went to bed at half past seven
Now we're sure we're going to Heaven

And then we rose
At half past six
And crumpled the paper
To burn the sticks.

And when we went to put on the logs
The fire was so hot that it roasted us hogs.

> (Evidently the last rhyme is put in
> purely for the sake of the rhyme!
>   T.R.)

Good morning Mr. President,
How are you to-day,
We have obeyed your orders,
We're very glad to say,
We went around the White House,
Araisin up a row,
And if you want to know about it,
Then We'll tell you now.

We went into the East Room,
We went into the Red.
And frightened everyone,
Who was not in his bed.

We want to have a pillar fight,
With you this very night,
And if you do not play with us,
We'll squeeze you very tight.

>   (signed)
>   Archie Roosevelt
>   Nicholas Roosevelt

TED'S SPRAINED ANKLE

White House, Nov. 28, 1903.

DEAR TED:

If I were you I should certainly get the best ankle support possible. You do not want to find next fall that Webb* beats you for end because your ankle gives out and his does not. If I were in your place, if it were necessary, I should put the ankle in plaster for the next three weeks, or for as long as the doctor thinks it needful, rather than run any risk of this. At any rate, I would consult him and wear whatever he thinks is the right thing.

· ·

I wonder if you are old enough yet to care for a good history of the American Revolution. If so, I think I shall give you mine by Sir George Trevelyan; although it is by an Englishman, I really think it on the whole the best account I have read. If I give it to you you must be very careful of it, because he sent it to me himself.

P.S.—The Bond parrot for mother has turned up; it is a most meritorious parrot, very friendly, and quite a remarkable talker.

THE SUPREME CHRISTMAS JOY
(To his sister, Mrs. Douglas Robinson)

White House, Dec. 26, 1903.

· ·

We had a delightful Christmas yesterday—just such a Christmas thirty or forty years ago we used to have under Father's and

*W. Seward Webb, Groton School student in the class of 1905, one year ahead of Ted.

Mother's supervision in 20th street and 57th street. At seven all the children came in to open the big, bulgy stockings in our bed; Kermit's terrier, Allan, a most friendly little dog, adding to the children's delight by occupying the middle of the bed. From Alice to Quentin, each child was absorbed in his or her stocking, and Edith certainly managed to get the most wonderful stocking toys. Bob was in looking on, and Aunt Emily, of course. Then, after breakfast, we all formed up and went into the library, where bigger toys were on separate tables for the children. I wonder whether there ever can come in life a thrill of greater exaltation and rapture than that which comes to one between the ages of say six and fourteen, when the library door is thrown open and you walk in to see all the gifts, like a materialized fairy land, arrayed on your special table?

. . . .

A DAY WITH A JUGGLER

White House, Jan. 18, 1904.

DEAR KERMIT:

Thursday and Friday there was a great deal of snow on the ground, and the weather was cold, so that Mother and I had two delightful rides up Rock Creek. The horses were clipped and fresh, and we were able to let them go along at a gallop, while the country was wonderfully beautiful.

To-day, after lunch, Mother took Ethel, Archie and Quentin, each with a friend, to see some most wonderful juggling and sleight of hand tricks by Kellar.* I went along and was as much in-

*Harry Kellar, outstanding magician in America at turn of the century.

terested as any of the children, though I had to come back to my work in the office before it was half through. At one period Ethel gave up her ring for one of the tricks. It was mixed up with the rings of five other little girls, and then all six rings were apparently pounded up and put into a pistol and shot into a collection of boxes, where five of them were subsequently found, each tied around a rose. Ethel's, however, had disappeared, and he made believe that it had vanished, but at the end of the next trick a remarkable bottle, out of which many different liquids had been poured, suddenly developed a delightful white guinea pig, squirming and kicking and looking exactly like Admiral Dewey, with around its neck Ethel's ring, tied by a pink ribbon. Then it was wrapped up in a paper, handed to Ethel; and when Ethel opened it, behold, there was no guinea pig, but a bunch of roses with a ring.

MERITS OF MILITARY AND CIVIL LIFE

White House, Jan. 21, 1904.

DEAR TED:

This will be a long business letter. I sent to you the examination papers for West Point and Annapolis. I have thought a great deal over the matter, and discussed it at great length with Mother. I feel on the one hand that I ought to give you my best advice, and yet on the other hand I do not wish to seem to constrain you against your wishes. If you have definitely made up your mind that you have an overmastering desire to be in the Navy or the Army, and that such a career is the one in which you will take a really heart-felt interest—far more so than any other—and that your greatest chance for happiness and usefulness will lie in doing this one work to which you feel yourself especially drawn—why, under such circumstances, I have but little to say. But I am not satisfied that this is really your feeling. It seemed to me more as if you did not feel drawn in any other direction, and wondered what you were going to do in life or what kind of work you would turn your hand to, and wondered if you could make a success or not; and that you are therefore inclined to turn to the Navy or Army chiefly because you would then have a definite and settled career in life, and could hope to go on steadily without any great risk of failure. Now, if such is your thought, I shall quote to you what Captain Mahan* said of his son when asked why he did not send him to West Point or Annapolis. "I have too much confidence in him to make me feel that it is desirable for him to enter either branch of the service."

I have great confidence in you. I believe you have the ability and, above all, the energy, the perseverance, and the common sense, to win out in civil life. That you will have some hard times and some discouraging times I have no question; but this is merely another way of saying that you will share the common lot. Though you will have to work in different ways from those in which I worked, you will not have to work any harder, nor to face periods of more dis-couragement. I trust in your ability, and especially your character, and I am confident you will win.

In the Army and the Navy the chance for a man to show great ability and rise above his fellows does not occur on the average

---

*Alfred Thayer Mahan, naval officer and author of influential works on naval policy and history greatly admired by TR.

more than once in a generation. When I was down at Santiago it was melancholy for me to see how fossilized and lacking in ambition, and generally useless, were most of the men of my age and over, who had served their lives in the Army. The Navy for the last few years has been better, but for twenty years after the Civil War there was less chance in the Navy than in the Army to practise, and do, work of real consequence. I have actually known lieutenants in both the Army and the Navy who were grandfathers—men who had seen their children married before they themselves attained the grade of captain. Of course the chance may come at any time when the man of West Point or Annapolis who will have stayed in the Army or Navy finds a great war on, and therefore has the opportunity to rise high. Under such circumstances, I think that the man of such training who has actually left the Army or the Navy has even more chance of rising than the man who has remained in it. Moreover, often a man can do as I did in the Spanish War, even though not a West Pointer.

This last point raises the question about you going to West Point or Annapolis and leaving the Army or Navy after you have served the regulation four years (I think that is the number) after graduation from the academy. Under this plan you would have an excellent education and a grounding in discipline and, in some ways, a testing of your capacity greater than I think you can get in any ordinary college. On the other hand, except for the profession of an engineer, you would have had nothing like special training, and you would be so ordered about, and arranged for, that you would have less independence of character than you could gain from them. You would have had fewer temptations; but you would have had less chance to develop the qualities which overcome temptations and show that a man has individual initiative.

Supposing you entered at seventeen, with the intention of following this course. The result would be that at twenty-five you would leave the Army or Navy without having gone through any law school or any special technical school of any kind, and would start your life work three or four years later than your schoolfellows of to-day, who go to work immediately after leaving college. Of course, under such circumstances, you might study law, for instance, during the four years after graduation; but my own feeling is that a man does good work chiefly when he is in something which he intends to make his permanent work, and in which he is deeply interested. Moreover, there will always be the chance that the number of officers in the Army or Navy will be deficient, and that you would have to stay in the service instead of getting out when you wished.

I want you to think over all these matters very seriously. It would be a great misfortune for you to start into the Army or Navy as a career, and find that you had mistaken your desires and had gone in without really weighing the matter.

You ought not to enter unless you feel genuinely drawn to the life as a life-work. If so, go in; but not otherwise.

Mr. Loeb told me to-day that at 17 he had tried for the army, but failed. The competitor who beat him in is now a captain; Mr. Loeb has passed him by, although meanwhile a war has been fought. Mr. Loeb says he wished to enter the army because he did not know what to do, could not foresee whether he would succeed or fail in life, and felt the army would give him "a living and a career." Now if this is at bottom your feeling I should advise you not to go in; I should say yes to some boys, but not to you; I believe in you too much, and have too much confidence in you.

ROOT AND TAFT

White House, Feb. 6, 1904.

DEAR TED:

I was glad to hear that you were to be confirmed.

Secretary Root* left on Monday and Governor Taft† took his place. I have missed, and shall miss, Root dreadfully. He has been the ablest, most generous and most disinterested friend and adviser that any President could hope to have; and immediately after leaving he rendered me a great service by a speech at the Union League Club, in which he said in most effective fashion the very things I should have liked him to say; and his words, moreover, carried weight as the words of no other man at this time addressing such an audience could have done. Taft is a splendid fellow and will be an aid and comfort in every way. But, as mother says, he is too much like me to be able to give me as good advice as Mr. Root was able to do because of the very differences of character between us.

If after fully thinking the matter over you remain firmly convinced that you want to go into the army, well and good. I shall be rather sorry for your decision, because I have great confidence in you and I believe that in civil life you could probably win in the end a greater prize than will be open to you if you go into the army— though, of course, a man can do well in the army. I know perfectly well that you will have hard times in civil life. Probably most young

*Elihu Root, American statesman and both secretary of war and later secretary of state in TR's cabinet.

†William Howard Taft, governor general of the Philippines, succeeded Root as secretary of war. He was TR's handpicked choice to follow him as president, and later became chief justice of the United States.

fellows when they have graduated from college, or from their post-graduate course, if they take any, feel pretty dismal for the first few years. In ordinary cases it at first seems as if their efforts were not leading anywhere, as if the pressure around the foot of the ladder was too great to permit of getting up to the top. But I have faith in your energy, your perseverance, your ability, and your power to force yourself to the front when you have once found out and taken your line. However, you and I and mother will talk the whole matter over when you come back here on Easter.

SENATOR HANNA'S DEATH

White House, Feb. 19, 1904.

DEAR TED:

Poor Hanna's* death was a tragedy. At the end he wrote me a note, the last he ever wrote, which showed him at his best, and which I much appreciate. His death was very sad for his family and close friends, for he had many large and generous traits, and had made a great success in life by his energy, perseverance and burly strength.

Buffalo Bill† was at lunch the other day, together with John Willis‡ my old hunter. Buffalo Bill has always been a great friend of mine. I remember when I was running for Vice-President I struck

---

*Senator Marcus A. "Mark" Hanna, political boss of Ohio who helped McKinley attain the presidency. He called TR "that damned cowboy" when he took over the White House, but later became his friend.

†Colonel William Frederick Cody, colorful frontiersman, scout, and Indian fighter, who starred in his original Wild West show.

‡John Willis, renowned hunter of bear in Montana and Idaho.

a Kansas town just when the Wild West show was there. He got upon the rear platform of my car and made a brief speech on my behalf, ending with the statement that "a cyclone from the West had come; no wonder the rats hunted their cellars!"

. . . .

As for you, I think the West Point education is, of course, good for any man, but I still think that you have too much in you for me to be glad to see you go into the Army, where in time of peace progress is so much a matter of routine.

IRRITATING REMARK BY QUENTIN

White House, Feb. 27, 1904.

DEAR KERMIT:

Mother went off for three days to New York and Mame and Quentin took instant advantage of her absence to fall sick. Quentin's sickness was surely due to a riot in candy and ice-cream with chocolate sauce. He was a very sad bunny next morning and spent a couple of days in bed. Ethel, as always, was as good as gold both to him and to Archie, and largely relieved me of my duties as vice-mother. I got up each morning in time to breakfast with Ethel and Archie before they started for school, and I read a certain amount to Quentin, but this was about all. I think Archie escaped with a minimum of washing for the three days. One day I asked him before Quentin how often he washed his face, whereupon Quentin interpolated, "very seldom, I fear," which naturally produced from Archie violent recriminations of a strongly personal type. Mother came back yesterday, having thoroughly enjoyed Parsifal. All the horses continue sick.

JAPANESE WRESTLING

White House, March 5, 1904.

DEAR KERMIT:

. . . .

I am wrestling with two Japanese wrestlers three times a week. I am not the age or the build one would think to be whirled lightly over an opponent's head and batted down on a mattress without damage. But they are so skilful that I have not been hurt at all. My throat is a little sore, because once when one of them had a strangle hold I also got hold of his windpipe and thought I could perhaps choke him off before he could choke me. However, he got ahead.

White House, April 9, 1904.

DEAR TED:

I am very glad I have been doing this Japanese wrestling, but when I am through with it this time I am not at all sure I shall ever try it again while I am so busy with other work as I am now. Often by the time I get to five o'clock in the afternoon I will be feeling like a stewed owl, after an eight hours' grapple with Senators, Congressmen, etc.; then I find the wrestling a trifle too vehement for mere rest. My right ankle and my left wrist and one thumb and both great toes are swollen sufficiently to more or less impair their usefulness, and I am well mottled with bruises elsewhere. Still I have made good progress, and since you left they have taught me three new throws that are perfect corkers.

LOVE FOR THE WHITE HOUSE

White House, May 28, 1904.

DEAR TED:

. . . .

I am having a reasonable amount of work and rather more than
a reasonable amount of worry. But, after all, life is lovely here. The
country is beautiful, and I do not think that any two people ever got
more enjoyment out of the White House than Mother and I. We
love the house itself, without and within, for its associations, for its
stillness and its simplicity. We love the garden. And we like Washington. We almost always take our breakfast on the south portico
now, Mother looking very pretty and dainty in her summer dresses.
Then we stroll about the garden for fifteen or twenty minutes,
looking at the flowers and the fountain and admiring the trees.
Then I work until between four and five, usually having some official people to lunch—now a couple of Senators, now a couple of
Ambassadors, now a literary man, now a capitalist or a labor leader,
or a scientist, or a big-game hunter. If Mother wants to ride, we
then spend a couple of hours on horseback. We had a lovely ride
up on the Virginia shore since I came back, and yesterday went up
Rock Creek and swung back home by the roads where the locust
trees were most numerous—for they are now white with blossoms.
It is the last great burst of bloom which we shall see this year except the laurels. But there are plenty of flowers in bloom or just
coming out, the honeysuckle most conspicuously. The south portico is fragrant with that now. The jasmine will be out later. If we
don't ride I walk or play tennis. But I am afraid Ted has gotten out
of his father's class in tennis!

PETER RABBIT'S FUNERAL

White House, May 28, 1904.

DEAR KERMIT:

It was great fun seeing you and Ted, and I enjoyed it to the full.

Ethel, Archie and Quentin have gone to Mount Vernon to-day with the Garfield boys. Yesterday poor Peter Rabbit died and his funeral was held with proper state. Archie, in his overalls, dragged the wagon with the little black coffin in which poor Peter Rabbit lay. Mother walked behind as chief mourner; she and Archie solemnly exchanging tributes to the worth and good qualities of the departed. Then he was buried, with a fuchsia over the little grave.

You remember Kenneth Grahame's account of how Harold went to the circus and sang the great spheral song of the circus? Well, yesterday Mother leaned out of her window and heard Archie, swinging under a magnolia tree, singing away to himself, "I'm going to Sagamore, to Sagamore, to Sagamore. I'm going to Sagamore, oh, to Sagamore!" It was his spheral song of joy and thanksgiving.

The children's delight at going to Sagamore next week has completely swallowed up all regret at leaving Mother and me. Quentin is very cunning. He and Archie love to play the hose into the sand-box and then, with their thigh rubber boots on, to get in and make fortifications. Now and then they play it over each other. Ethel is playing tennis quite a good deal.

I think Yagenka is going to come out all right, and Bleistein, too. I have no hope for Wyoming or Renown. Fortunately, Rusty is serving us well.

White House, June 12th, 1904.

BLESSED QUENTY-QUEE:

The little birds in the nest in the vines on the garden fence are nearly grown up. Their mother still feeds them.

You see the mother bird with a worm in her beak, and the little birds with their beaks wide open!

I was out walking the other day and passed the Zoo; there I fed with grass some of the two-year-old elk; the bucks had their horns "in the velvet." I fed them through the bars.

White House, June 12th, 1904.

Blessed Archie-kins:

Give my love to Mademoiselle*; I hope you and Quenty are *very* good with her—and don't play in the library!

I loved your letter, and think you were very good to write.

All kinds of live things are sent me from time to time. The other day an eagle came; this morning an owl.

(I have drawn him holding a rat in one claw.)

We sent both to the Zoo.

The other day while walking with Mr. Pinchot† and Mr. Garfield‡ we climbed into the Blagden deer park and almost walked over such a pretty wee fawn, all spotted; it ran off like a little race horse.

*Regine Drolet, governess to Archie and Quentin.

†Gifford Pinchot, appointed by TR the first chief of the Bureau of Forestry, later became governor of Pennsylvania.

‡James Randolph Garfield, secretary of the interior in TR's cabinet 1907–1909, after serving on the Civil Service Commission and as commissioner of corporations.

It made great jumps and held its white tail straight in the air.

White House, June 21, 1904.

DEAR QUENTYQUEE:

The other day when out riding what should I see in the road ahead of me but a real B'rer Terrapin and B'rer Rabbit. They were sitting solemnly beside one another and looked just as if they had come out of a book; but as my horse walked along B'rer Rabbit went lippity lippity lippity off into the bushes and B'rer Terrapin drew in his head and legs till I passed.

LIFE WITH FATHER

Edith's 1894 photograph of TR playing a strenuous game of
ball with his family shows Father doing what he liked best,
romping with his children and their cousins at his beloved
Sagamore Hill. His enthusiasm for this home was shared by them
all. Little Archie was heard one spring day singing to himself
from the branches of a White House tree: "I'm going to Sagamore,
to Sagamore, to Sagamore. I'm going to Sagamore, oh, to Sagamore!"

Sagamore in winter. The dogs enjoy the
snow as much as the family.

Ted napping on
a bearskin. Someone
has mischievously placed
the bear paws on his back.

Sagamore in summer. Archie, resplendent in straw boater, strikes off on his own down the walk.

SAGAMORE HILL NATIONAL HISTORIC SITE

The North Room, filled with Father's treasures, spelled romance to the children.

LIBRARY OF CONGRESS

SAGAMORE HILL NATIONAL HISTORIC SITE

Ethel fearlessly cuddling a wolf's unfriendly head.

Quentin atop the icehouse, located just outside the kitchen door.

Cousin Philip (*left*) and Quentin straddling the ridgepole. Edith said she "had a shock" when she first saw this picture of her youngest.

Archie balancing on Cousin Nick's shoulders.

Quentin and Archie on the windmill, the favorite climbing place of all the young Roosevelts.

Father timing a handicap race around the old barn before an appreciative audience.

TR leading
Archie, Edith,
and Quentin on
a brisk hike
through the
fields surround-
ing Sagamore.

Archie (*left*) and his friend Henry Landon sailing on Long Island Sound.

Ted and Cousin John exploring the marshes. Ted wears a slouch hat to look like his father.

Cooper's Bluff, two hundred terrifying feet down to the sound.

A Family of Riders

Booted and spurred, Father and family set out for the daily early morning ride.

Father takes Bleistein over a fence: "Not a purty rider, but a hell of a *good* rider."

Alice, in comparison with TR, cuts a picture of elegance.

Edith, astride Yagenka,
rides sidesaddle,
as do her daughters.

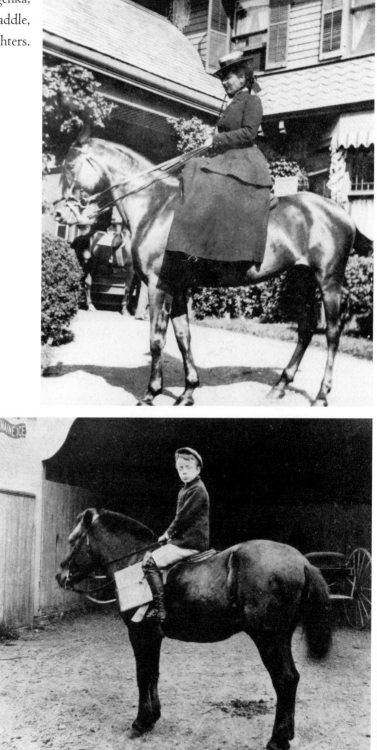

Ted, on pony
Grant, heads to
the village for
his piano
lesson.

Kermit and mount, both beautifully turned out.

Ethel enjoying a country ride with a friend.

Archie, decked out in western gear, on his beloved pony Algonquin.

Quentin manages to keep the egg in the spoon during a headlong race.

Mother with Ethel, Kermit, Ted, and Alice on the dock at Fleet's Pond, in an 1895 photograph probably taken by Father.

Three Roosevelt children on the shore at Oyster Bay.

Quentin searching for June bugs in the daisy fields.

Mame with Ethel and Kermit taking a ride in the pony cart.

Quentin and Archie blowing soap bubbles.

Ted, Ethel, Kermit, and Alice bedecked for a fancy dress ball.

Ethel and Alice surrounded by dolls, which they rarely played with.

Archie, done up like a little princess, photographed with *his* doll.

Mother, as was her custom, reads to Archie and Quentin before dinner.

Father, with Skip in his arms, enjoys the sun and a book at the
ranch house in West Divide Creek, Colorado.

Five-year-old Ted poring over a book in the family library.

Alice started reading at an early age and never stopped:
"My father read all the time, so I just followed his example."

Kermit and Ethel deep in their books while Father chats with Mother.
England, 1910, following the African safari.

Family Pets

Archie, Ethel, and Cousin Philip relax in the sun with seven
"Heinz pickle" dogs at Sagamore Hill.

The photographer Edward Curtis took this picture of himself with Quentin,
Archie, and Cousin Nicholas burying one of the Sagamore dogs.

Kermit, Ethel, and Ted with some of their guinea pigs.

Quentin feeding his rabbits.

Archie clutching his plump badger Josiah.

Archie with Skip.

Like Father, Like Son

Ted, age three, with his father.

Thirteen-year-old Ted with his first buck.

TR shooting a big bear out of a tree.

ROOSEVELT COLLECTION, HARVARD

Ethel, Ted, Kermit, and Alice visit the Rough Riders at their camp at Montauk Point. Father stands between Kermit and Alice.

AMERICAN MUSEUM OF NATURAL HISTORY (ZA6145)

Father carried this picture of his children, given to him by Edith, through the war in Cuba. Quentin had not been born when it was taken.

Twelve Cousins by Height

It was a family custom to line up as many of the young of the Roosevelt clan as possible and take their pictures each year by height and age.

Twelve Cousins by Age

Groton

Hundred House, Groton's main building.

The four Roosevelt boys occupied a spartan dormitory such as this in
"the most exclusive school in America."

President Roosevelt arriving at the Ayer train station in 1904 to give the twentieth-anniversary address at Groton. With him are headmaster Endicott Peabody (*left*) and Kermit.

The headmaster and TR make a snappy entrance to the school grounds.

Ethel, sixteen, and her mother make an elegant duo in their summer frocks.

Flanked by her new husband, Congressman Nicholas Longworth, and her father, the president, Alice enjoyed a dazzling White House wedding in 1906.

TR proudly escorts Ethel into Christ Church in Oyster Bay for her wedding to Dr. Richard Derby in 1913.

A somber Roosevelt family poses on the porch for a last
White House photograph in March 1909.

Off to Africa

Aboard the S.S. *Hamburg* bound for Africa, TR watches Kermit (*left*) jousting on a greased log. (From an album originally owned by Captain Erwin Kornitzer, second officer.)

Loving Grandfather

We Fight To Make The World A Decent Place For Our Children To Live In.

At his death in 1919, TR had eight grandchildren and had been photographed with most of them. His favorite photo was this one, taken by Clarence LeGendre of *The World Magazine*, of himself and little Edith Roosevelt Derby in 1918.

CHARMS OF VALLEY FORGE

White House, June 21, 1904.

DEAREST ETHEL:

I think you are a little trump and I love your letter, and the way you take care of the children and keep down the expenses and cook bread and are just your own blessed busy cunning self. You would have enjoyed being at Valley Forge with us on Sunday. It is a beautiful place, and, of course, full of historic associations. The garden here is lovely. A pair of warbling vireos have built in a linden and sing all the time. The lindens, by the way, are in bloom, and Massachusetts Avenue is fragrant with them. The magnolias are all in bloom, too, and the jasmine on the porch.

WASHINGTON'S COMPANIONS AT VALLEY FORGE

White House, June 21, 1904.

DEAR TED:

Mother and I had a most lovely ride the other day, way up beyond Sligo Creek to what is called North-west Branch, at Burnt Mills, where is a beautiful gorge, deep and narrow, with great boulders and even cliffs. Excepting Great Falls it is the most beautiful place around here. Mother scrambled among the cliffs in her riding habit, very pretty and most interesting. The roads were good and some of the scenery really beautiful. We were gone four hours, half an hour being occupied with the scrambling in the gorge.

Saturday we went to the wedding of Teddy Douglas* and Helen.* It was a beautiful wedding in every way and I am very fond of both of them. Sunday we spent at Attorney-General Knox's† at Valley Forge, and most unexpectedly I had to deliver a little address at the church in the afternoon, as they are trying to build a memorial to Washington. Think of the fact that in Washington's army that winter among the junior officers were Alexander Hamilton, Monroe and Marshall—a future President of the United States, the future Chief Justice who was to do such wonderful work for our Government, and the man of most brilliant mind—Hamilton—whom we have ever developed in this country.

ON THE EVE OF NOMINATION FOR PRESIDENT

White House, June 21, 1904.

DEAR KERMIT:

We spent to-day at the Knoxes'. It is a beautiful farm—just such a one as you could run. Phil Knox, as capable and efficient as he is diminutive, amused Mother and me greatly by the silent way in which he did in first-rate way his full share of all the work.

To-morrow the National Convention meets, and barring a cat-

---

*Theodore Douglas Robinson, son of TR's sister Corinne, married his sixth cousin, Helen Rebecca Roosevelt, daughter of James Roosevelt and Helen Schermerhorn (Astor) Roosevelt. Teddy Robinson was in the New York legislature and like TR served as assistant secretary of the Navy.

†Philander Chase Knox resigned as attorney general the year this letter was written and later became President Taft's secretary of state.

aclysm I shall be nominated. There is a great deal of sullen grumbling, but it has taken more the form of resentment against what they think is my dictation as to details than against me personally. They don't dare to oppose me for the nomination and I suppose it is hardly likely the attempt will be made to stampede the Convention for any one. How the election will turn out no man can tell. Of course I hope to be elected, but I realize to the full how very lucky I have been, not only to be President but to have been able to accomplish so much while President, and whatever may be the outcome, I am not only content but very sincerely thankful for all the good fortune I have had. From Panama down I have been able to accomplish certain things which will be of lasting importance in our history. Incidentally, I don't think that any family has ever enjoyed the White House more than we have. I was thinking about it just this morning when Mother and I took breakfast on the portico and afterwards walked about the lovely grounds and looked at the stately historic old house. It is a wonderful privilege to have been here and to have been given the chance to do this work, and I should regard myself as having a small and mean mind if in the event of defeat I felt soured at not having had more instead of being thankful for having had so much.

BILL THE LIZARD

White House, June 21, 1904.

BLESSED ARCHIKINS:

The other day when Mother and I were walking down the steps of the big south porch we saw a movement among the honeysuckles and there was Bill the lizard—your lizard that you brought home from Mount Vernon. We have seen him several times since and he is evidently entirely at home here. The White House seems big and empty without any of you children puttering around it, and I think the ushers miss you very much. I play tennis in the late afternoons unless I go to ride with Mother.

ON THE EVE OF ELECTION

White House, Oct. 15, 1904.

DARLING KERMIT:

The weather has been beautiful the last week—mild, and yet with the true feeling of Fall in the air. When Mother and I have ridden up Rock Creek through the country round about, it has been a perpetual delight just to look at the foliage. I have never seen leaves turn more beautifully. The Virginia creepers and some of the maple and gum trees are scarlet and crimson. The oaks are deep red brown. The beeches, birches and hickories are brilliant saffron. Just at this moment I am dictating while on my way with Mother to the wedding of Senator Knox's daughter, and the country is a blaze of color as we pass through it, so that it is a joy to the eye to look upon it. I do not think I have ever before seen the colorings of the woods so beautiful so far south as this. Ted is hard at work with Matt. Hale,* who is a very nice fellow and has become quite one of the household, like good Mademoiselle. I am really fond of her. She is so bright and amusing and now seems perfectly happy, and is not only devoted to Archie and Quentin but is very wise in the way she

---

*Matthew Hale, Ted's tutor, later a Boston lawyer. He was a relative of TR's first wife, Alice Hathaway Lee, and was state chairman of the Progressive party in Massachusetts.

takes care of them. Quentin, under parental duress, rides Algonquin every day. Archie has just bought himself a football suit, but I have not noticed that he has played football as yet. He is spending Saturday and Sunday out at Dr. Rixey's. Ted plays tennis with Matt. Hale and me and Mr. Cooley.* We tried Dan Moore.† You could beat him. Yesterday I took an afternoon off and we all went for a scramble and climb down the other side of the Potomac from Chain Bridge home. It was great fun. To-morrow (Sunday) we shall have lunch early and spend the afternoon in a drive of the entire family, including Ethel, but not including Archie and Quentin, out to Burnt Mills and back. When I say we all scrambled along the Potomac, I of course only meant Matt. Hale and Ted and I. Three or four active male friends took the walk with us.

In politics things at the moment seem to look quite right, but every form of lie is being circulated by the Democrats, and they intend undoubtedly to spring all kinds of sensational untruths at the very end of the campaign. I have not any idea whether we will win or not. Before election I shall send you my guess as to the way the different States will vote, and then you can keep it and see how near to the truth I come. But of course you will remember that it is a mere guess, and that I may be utterly mistaken all along the line. In any event, even if I am beaten you must remember that we have had three years of great enjoyment out of the Presidency and that we are mighty lucky to have had them.

I generally have people in to lunch, but at dinner, thank fortune, we are usually alone. Though I have callers in the evening, I gener-

---

*Alford Warriner Cooley, assistant attorney general under TR.
†Daniel Tyler Moore, Edith's first cousin and one of TR's military aides. As a sparring partner, Dan Moore landed the blow that left TR blind in one eye.

ally have an hour in which to sit with Mother and the others up in the library, talking and reading and watching the bright wood fire. Ted and Ethel, as well as Archie and Quentin, are generally in Mother's room for twenty minutes or a half hour just before she dresses, according to immemorial custom.

Last evening Mother and I and Ted and Ethel and Matt. Hale went to the theatre to see "The Yankee Consul," which was quite funny.

BIG JIM WHITE

White House, Dec. 3, 1904.

BLESSED KERMIT:

The other day while Major Loeffler* was marshalling the usual stream of visitors from England, Germany, the Pacific slope, etc., of warm admirers from remote country places, of bridal couples, etc., etc., a huge man about six feet four, of middle age, but with every one of his great sinews and muscles as fit as ever, came in and asked to see me on the ground that he was a former friend. As the line passed he was introduced to me as Mr. White. I greeted him in the usual rather perfunctory manner, and the huge, rough-looking fellow shyly remarked, "Mr. Roosevelt, maybe you don't recollect me. I worked on the roundup with you twenty years ago next spring. My outfit joined yours at the mouth of the Box Alder." I gazed at him, and at once said, "Why it is big Jim." He was a great cowpuncher and is still riding the range in northwestern Nebraska. When I knew him he was a tremendous fighting man, but always liked me. Twice I had to interfere to prevent him from half mur-

*Major Charles Loeffler, a Civil War veteran, was a White House receptionist.

dering cowboys from my own ranch. I had him at lunch, with a mixed company of home and foreign notabilities.

Don't worry about the lessons, old boy. I know you are studying hard. Don't get cast down. Sometimes in life, both at school and afterwards, fortune will go against any one, but if he just keeps pegging away and doesn't lose his courage things always take a turn for the better in the end.

WINTER LIFE IN THE WHITE HOUSE

White House, Dec. 17, 1904.

BLESSED KERMIT:

For a week the weather has been cold—down to zero at night and rarely above freezing in the shade at noon. In consequence the snow has lain well, and as there has been a waxing moon I have had the most delightful evening and night rides imaginable. I have been so busy that I have been unable to get away until after dark, but I went in the fur jacket Uncle Will presented to me as the fruit of his prize money in the Spanish War; and the moonlight on the glittering snow made the rides lovelier than they would have been in the daytime. Sometimes Mother and Ted went with me, and the gallops were delightful. To-day it has snowed heavily again, but the snow has been so soft that I did not like to go out, and besides I have been worked up to the limit. There has been skating and sleigh-riding all the week.

The new black "Jack" dog is becoming very much at home and very fond of the family.

With Archie and Quentin I have finished "The Last of the Mohicans," and have now begun "The Deerslayer." They are as cunning as ever, and this reading to them in the evening gives me a chance to see them that I would not otherwise have, although sometimes it is rather hard to get time.

Mother looks very young and pretty. This afternoon she was most busy, taking the little boys to the theatre and then going to hear Ethel sing. Ted, very swell in his first tail coat, is going out to take supper at Secretary Morton's,* whose pretty daughter is coming out to-night.

In a very few days now we shall see you again.

PLAYMATE OF THE CHILDREN
(To Mr. and Mrs. Emlen Roosevelt)[†]

White House, Jan. 4, 1905.

I am really touched at the way in which your children as well as my own treat me as a friend and playmate. It has its comic side. Thus, the last day the boys were here they were all bent upon having me take them for a scramble down Rock Creek. Of course, there was absolutely no reason why they could not go alone, but they obviously felt that my presence was needed to give zest to the entertainment. Accordingly, off I went, with the two Russell boys, George, Jack, and Philip, and Ted, Kermit, and Archie, with one of Archie's friends—a sturdy little boy who, as Archie informed me, had played opposite to him in the position of centre rush last fall. I do not think that one of them saw anything incongruous in the President's getting as bedaubed with mud as they got, or in my wig-

---

*Paul Morton, prominent businessman, appointed secretary of the Navy by TR in 1904.
[†]W. Emlen Roosevelt, or "Cousin Emlen," and his wife, "Cousin Christine" Roosevelt. Emlen looked after TR's business affairs when he was president and headed the Wall Street family firm of Roosevelt & Son.

gling and clambering around jutting rocks, through cracks, and up what were really small cliff faces, just like the rest of them; and whenever any one of them beat me at any point, he felt and expressed simple and whole-hearted delight, exactly as if it had been a triumph over a rival of his own age.

A JAPANESE BOY'S LETTER
(To Dr. William Sturgis Bigelow)*

White House, Jan. 14, 1905.

DEAR STURGIS:

Last year, when I had Professor Yamashita[†] teach me the "Jiudo"—as they seem now to call Jiu Jitsu—the naval attaché here, Commander Takashita, used to come around here and bring a young lad, Kitgaki, who is now entering Annapolis. I used to wrestle with them both. They were very fond of Archie and were very good to him. This Christmas Kitgaki sent from Annapolis a little present to Archie, who wrote to thank him, and Kitgaki sent him a letter back that we like so much that I thought you might enjoy it, as it shows so nice a trait in the Japanese character. It runs as follows:

My dearest boy:

I received your nice letter. I thank you ever so much. I am very very glad that you have receive my small present.

*Dr. William Sturgis Bigelow, Boston friend of TR's who spent many years in the Orient and became a Buddhist and collector of Oriental art.
†Professor Yamashita, an intellectual and exponent of jiujitsu.

I like you very very much. When I have been in Jiudo room with your father and you, your father was talking to us about the picture of the caverly officer. In that time, I saw some expression on your face. Another remembering of you is your bravery when you sleped down from a tall chair. The two rememberings can't leave from my head.

I returned here last Thursday and have plenty lesson, so my work is hard, hard, hard, more than Jiudo.

I hope your good health.

I am,

Sincerely yours,

A. KITGAKI.

Isn't it a nice letter?

ON COUNTING DAYS AND WRESTLING

White House, Feb. 24, 1905.

DARLING KERMIT:

I puzzled a good deal over your marks. I am inclined to think that one explanation is that you have thought so much of home as to prevent your really putting your whole strength into your studies. It is most natural that you should count the days before coming home, and write as you do that it will only be 33 days, only 26 days, only 19 days, etc., but at the same time it seems to me that perhaps this means that you do not really put all your heart and all your head effort into your work; and that if you are able to, it would be far better to think just as little as possible about coming home and resolutely set yourself to putting your best thought into your work. It is an illustration of the old adage about putting your hand to the plow and then looking back. In after life, of course, it is always possible that at some time you may have to go away for a year or two from home to do some piece of work. If during that whole time you only thought day after day of how soon you would get home I think you would find it difficult to do your best work; and maybe this feeling may be partly responsible for the trouble with the lessons at school.

Wednesday, Washington's Birthday, I went to Philadelphia and made a speech at the University of Pennsylvania, took lunch with the Philadelphia City Troop and came home the same afternoon with less fatigue than most of my trips cost me; for I was able to dodge the awful evening banquet and the night on the train which taken together drive me nearly melancholy mad. Since Sunday we have not been able to ride. I still box with Grant,* who has now become the champion middleweight wrestler of the United States. Yesterday afternoon we had Professor Yamashita up here to wrestle with Grant. It was very interesting, but of course jiu jitsu and our wrestling are so far apart that it is difficult to make any comparison between them. Wrestling is simply a sport with rules almost as conventional as those of tennis, while jiu jitsu is really meant for practice in killing or disabling our adversary. In consequence, Grant did not know what to do except to put Yamashita on his back, and Yamashita was perfectly content to be on his back. Inside of a minute Yamashita had choked Grant, and inside of two minutes more he got an elbow hold on him that would have enabled him to break his arm; so that there is no question but that he could have put Grant out. So far this made it evident that the jiu jitsu man could handle

*Joe Grant, champion wrestler and frequent opponent of TR's.

the ordinary wrestler. But Grant, in the actual wrestling and throwing was about as good as the Japanese, and he was so much stronger that he evidently hurt and wore out the Japanese. With a little practice in the art I am sure that one of our big wrestlers or boxers, simply because of his greatly superior strength, would be able to kill any of those Japanese, who though very good men for their inches and pounds are altogether too small to hold their own against big, powerful, quick men who are as well trained.

SPRING IN WASHINGTON

White House, March 20, 1905.

DEAR KERMIT:

Poor John Hay has been pretty sick. He is going away to try to pick up his health by a sea voyage and rest. I earnestly hope he succeeds, not only because of my great personal fondness for him, but because from the standpoint of the nation it would be very difficult to replace him. Every Sunday on my way home from church I have been accustomed to stop in and see him. The conversation with him was always delightful, and during these Sunday morning talks we often decided important questions of public policy.

I paid a scuttling visit to New York on Friday to give away Eleanor* at her marriage, and to make two speeches—one to the Friendly Sons of St. Patrick and one to the Sons of the American Revolution.

*Eleanor Roosevelt, daughter of TR's brother Elliott, married Franklin Delano Roosevelt, her father's fifth cousin, on March 17, 1903.

Mother and I have been riding a good deal, and the country is now lovely. Moreover, Ted and Matt and I have begun playing tennis.

The birds have come back. Not only song-sparrows and robins, but a winter wren, purple finches and tufted titmice are singing in the garden; and the other morning early Mother and I were waked up by the loud singing of a cardinal bird in the magnolia tree just outside our windows.

Yesterday afternoon Archie and Quentin each had a little boy to see him. They climbed trees, sailed boats in the fountain, and dug in the sandbox like woodcocks.

Poor Mr. Frank Travers* died last night. I was very sorry. He has been a good friend to me.

A HUNTING TRIP

Colorado Springs, Colorado, April 14, 1905.

BLESSED KERMIT:

I hope you had as successful a trip in Florida as I have had in Texas and Oklahoma. The first six days were of the usual Presidential tour type, but much more pleasant than ordinarily, because I did not have to do quite as much speaking, and there was a certain irresponsibility about it all, due I suppose in part to the fact that I am no longer a candidate and am free from the everlasting suspicion and ill-natured judgment which being a candidate entails. However, both in Kentucky, and especially in Texas, I was received with a warmth and heartiness that surprised me,

---

*Frank Travers, a merchant, was a Roosevelt neighbor in Oyster Bay.

while the Rough Riders' reunion at San Antonio was delightful in every way.

Then came the five days wolf hunting in Oklahoma, and this was unalloyed pleasure, except for my uneasiness about Auntie Bye and poor little Sheffield. General Young,[*] Dr. Lambert[†] and Roly Fortescue[‡] were each in his own way just the nicest companions imaginable, my Texas hosts were too kind and friendly and open-hearted for anything. I want to have the whole party up at Washington next winter. The party got seventeen wolves, three coons, and any number of rattlesnakes. I was in at the death of eleven wolves. The other six wolves were killed by members of the party who were off with bunches of dogs in some place where I was not. I never took part in a run which ended in the death of a wolf without getting through the run in time to see the death. It was tremendous galloping over cut banks, prairie dog towns, flats, creek bottoms, everything. One run was nine miles long and I was the only man in at the finish except the professional wolf hunter Abernathy,[§] who is a really wonderful fellow, catching the wolves alive by thrusting his gloved hands down between their jaws so that they cannot bite. He caught one wolf alive, tied up this wolf, and then held it on the saddle, followed his dogs in a seven-mile run and helped kill another wolf. He has a pretty wife and five cunning chil-

---

[*]Brigadier General S.B.M. Young, under whom TR served in the Spanish-American War and whom he promoted to lieutenant general when he was president.

[†]Dr. Alexander Lambert, physician and lifelong friend of TR. He took the photographs that illustrate TR's *Outdoor Pastimes of an American Hunter.*

[‡]Granville Roland "Roly" Fortescue, who served in the Rough Riders and remained in the Army until 1906, when he became a war correspondent. He was the illegitimate son of TR's uncle, Robert B. Roosevelt.

[§]John "Jack" Abernathy, Oklahoma rancher and hunter.

dren of whom he is very proud, and introduced them to me, and I liked him much. We were in the saddle eight or nine hours every day, and I am rather glad to have thirty-six hours' rest on the cars before starting on my Colorado bear hunt.

ABERNATHY THE WOLF HUNTER

Glenwood Springs, Colorado, April 20, 1905.

DEAR TED:

I do wish you could have been along on this trip. It has been great fun. In Oklahoma our party got all told seventeen coyotes with the greyhounds. I was in at the death of eleven, the only ones started by the dogs with which I happened to be. In one run the three Easterners covered themselves with glory, as Dr. Lambert, Roly Fortescue and I were the only ones who got through excepting Abernathy, the wolf hunter. It happened because it was a nine-mile run and all the cowboys rode their horses to a standstill in the first three or four miles, after which I came bounding along, like Kermit in the paper chase, and got to the end in time to see the really remarkable feat of Abernathy jumping on to the wolf, thrusting his gloved hand into its mouth, and mastering it then and there. He never used a knife or a rope in taking these wolves, seizing them by sheer quickness and address and thrusting his hand into the wolf's mouth in such a way that it lost all power to bite. You would have loved Tom Burnett, the son of the big cattle man. He is a splendid fellow, about thirty years old, and just the ideal of what a young cattle man should be.

Up here we have opened well. We have two cracker jacks as guides—John Goff, my old guide on the mountain lion hunt, and

Jake Borah, who has somewhat the Seth Bullock* type of face. We have about thirty dogs, including one absurd little terrier about half Jack's size, named Skip. Skip trots all day long with the hounds, excepting when he can persuade Mr. Stewart, or Dr. Lambert, or me to take him up for a ride, for which he is always begging. He is most affectionate and intelligent, but when there is a bear or lynx at bay he joins in the fight with all the fury of a bull dog, though I do not think he is much more effective than one of your Japanese mice would be. I should like to bring him home for Archie or Quentin. He would go everywhere with them and would ride Betsy or Algonquin.

On the third day out I got a fine big black bear, an old male who would not tree, but made what they call in Mississippi a walking bay with the dogs, fighting them off all the time. The chase lasted nearly two hours and was ended by a hard scramble up a canyon side; and I made a pretty good shot at him as he was walking off with the pack around him. He killed one dog and crippled three that I think will recover, besides scratching others. My 30–40 Springfield worked to perfection on the bear.

I suppose you are now in the thick of your studies and will have but little time to rest after the examinations. I shall be back about the 18th, and then we can take up our tennis again. Give my regards to Matt.

. . . .

*Seth Bullock, sheriff of the Black Hills district and longtime friend of TR, who later appointed him U.S. marshal for South Dakota.

PRAIRIE GIRLS

Divide Creek, Colo., April 26, 1905.

DARLING ETHEL:

Of course you remember the story of the little prairie girl. I always associate it with you. Well, again and again on this trip we would pass through prairie villages—bleak and lonely—with all the people in from miles about to see me. Among them were often dozens of young girls, often pretty, and as far as I could see much more happy than the heroine of the story. One of them shook hands with me, and then, after much whispering, said: "We want to shake hands with the guard!" The "guard" proved to be Roly, who was very swell in his uniform, and whom they evidently thought much more attractive than the President, both in age and looks.

There are plenty of ranchmen round here; they drive over to camp to see me, usually bringing a cake, or some milk and eggs, and are very nice and friendly. About twenty of the men came out with me, "to see the President shoot a bear"; and fortunately I did so in the course of an exhausting twelve hours' ride. I am very homesick for you all.

BEARS, BOBCATS AND SKIP

Glenwood Springs, Colorado, May 2, 1905.

BLESSED KERMIT:

I was delighted to get your letter. I am sorry you are having such a hard time in mathematics, but hope a couple of weeks will set you all right. We have had a very successful hunt. All told we have obtained ten bear and three bobcats. Dr. Lambert has been a perfect trump. He is in the pink of condition, while for the last week I have been a little knocked out by the Cuban fever. Up to that time I was simply in splendid shape. There is a very cunning little dog named Skip, belonging to John Goff's pack, who has completely adopted me. I think I shall take him home to Archie. He likes to ride on Dr. Lambert's horse, or mine, and though he is not as big as Jack, takes eager part in the fight with every bear and bobcat.

I am sure you will enjoy your trip to Deadwood with Seth Bullock, and as soon as you return from Groton I shall write to him about it. I have now become very homesick for Mother, and shall be glad when the 12th of May comes and I am back in the White House.

HOME AGAIN WITH SKIP

White House, May 14, 1905.

DEAR KERMIT:

Here I am back again, and mighty glad to be back. It was perfectly delightful to see Mother and the children, but it made me very homesick for you. Of course I was up to my ears in work as soon as I reached the White House, but in two or three days we shall be through it and can settle down into our old routine.

Yesterday afternoon we played tennis, Herbert Knox Smith* and I beating Matt and Murray.† To-day I shall take cunning mother out for a ride.

Skip accompanied me to Washington. He is not as yet entirely at home in the White House and rather clings to my companion-

---

*Herbert Knox Smith, lawyer from Connecticut appointed commissioner of corporations by TR.

†Lawrence O. Murray, assistant secretary of commerce and labor from 1904 to 1908, later appointed comptroller of the currency by TR.

ship. I think he will soon be fond of Archie, who loves him dearly. Mother is kind to Skip, but she does not think he is an aristocrat as Jack is. He is a very cunning little dog all the same.

Mother walked with me to church this morning and both the past evenings we have been able to go out into the garden and sit on the stone benches near the fountain. The country is too lovely for anything, everything being a deep, rich, fresh green.

I had a great time in Chicago with the labor union men. They made what I regarded as a rather insolent demand upon me, and I gave them some perfectly straight talk about their duty and about the preservation of law and order. The trouble seems to be increasing there, and I may have to send Federal troops into the city—though I shall not do so unless it is necessary.

SKIP IN THE WHITE HOUSE

White House, May 14, 1905.

DEAR KERMIT:

That was a good mark in Latin, and I am pleased with your steady improvement in it.

Skip is housebroken, but he is like a real little Indian. He can stand any amount of hard work if there is a bear or bobcat ahead, but now that he is in the White House he thinks he would much rather do nothing but sit about all day with his friends, and threatens to turn into a lapdog. But when we get him to Oyster Bay I think we can make him go out riding with us, and then I think he will be with Archie a great deal. He and Jack are rather jealous of one another. He is very cunning and friendly. I am immensely pleased with Mother's Virginia cottage and its name. I am going down there for Sunday with her some time soon.

P.S.—Your marks have just come! By George, you have worked hard and I am delighted. Three cheers!

OFFICERS OF TOGO'S FLEET

White House, June 6, 1905.

DEAR KERMIT:

Next Friday I am going down with Mother to spend a couple of days at Pine Knot, which Mother loves just as Ethel loves Fidelity. She and I have had some lovely rides together, and if I do not go riding with her I play tennis with Ted and some of his and my friends. Yesterday Ted and one of his friends played seven sets of tennis against Mr. Cooley and me and beat us four to three. In the evening Commander Takashita brought in half a dozen Japanese naval officers who had been with Togo's fleet off Port Arthur and had taken part in the fleet actions, the attacks with the torpedo-boat flotilla, and so forth. I tell you they were a formidable-looking set and evidently dead game fighters!

A PRESIDENT AS COOK

White House, June 11, 1905.

DEAR KERMIT:

Mother and I have just come home from a lovely trip to "Pine Knot." It is really a perfectly delightful little place; the nicest little place of the kind you can imagine. Mother is a great deal more pleased with it than any child with any toy I ever saw. She went down the day before, Thursday, and I followed on Friday morning.

Good Mr. Joe Wilmer met me at the station and we rode on horse-back to "Round Top," where we met Mother and Mr. Willie Wilmer. We all had tea there and then drove to "Plain Dealing," where we had dinner. Of course I loved both "Round Top" and "Plain Dealing," and as for the two Mr. Wilmers, they are the most generous, thoughtful, self-effacing friends that any one could wish to see. After dinner we went over to "Pine Knot," put everything to order and went to bed. Next day we spent all by ourselves at "Pine Knot." In the morning I fried bacon and eggs, while Mother boiled the kettle for tea and laid the table. Breakfast was most successful, and then Mother washed the dishes and did most of the work, while I did odd jobs. Then we walked about the place, which is fifteen acres in all, saw the lovely spring, admired the pine trees and the oak trees, and then Mother lay in the hammock while I cut away some trees to give us a better view from the piazza. The piazza is the real feature of the house. It is broad and runs along the whole length and the roof is high near the wall, for it is a continuation of the roof of the house. It was lovely to sit there in the rocking-chairs and hear all the birds by daytime and at night the whippoorwills and owls and little forest folk.

Inside the house is just a bare wall with one big room below, which is nice now, and will be still nicer when the chimneys are up and there is a fireplace in each end. A rough flight of stairs leads above, where there are two rooms, separated by a passageway. We did everything for ourselves, but all the food we had was sent over to us by the dear Wilmers, together with milk. We cooked it ourselves, so there was no one around the house to bother us at all. As we found that cleaning dishes took up an awful time we only took two meals a day, which was all we wanted. On Saturday evening I fried two chickens for dinner, while Mother boiled the tea, and we had cherries and wild strawberries, as well as biscuits and corn-bread. To my pleasure Mother greatly enjoyed the fried chicken and admitted that what you children had said of the way I fried chicken was all true. In the evening we sat out a long time on the piazza, and then read indoors and then went to bed. Sunday morning we did not get up until nine. Then I fried Mother some beefsteak and some eggs in two frying-pans, and she liked them both very much. We went to church at the dear little church where the Wilmers' father and mother had been married, dined soon after two at "Plain Dealing," and then were driven over to the station to go back to Washington. I rode the big black stallion—Chief—and enjoyed it thoroughly. Altogether we had a very nice holiday.

I was lucky to be able to get it, for during the past fortnight, and indeed for a considerable time before, I have been carrying on negotiations with both Russia and Japan, together with side negotiations with Germany, France and England, to try to get the present war stopped. With infinite labor and by the exercise of a good deal of tact and judgment—if I do say it myself—I have finally gotten the Japanese and Russians to agree to meet to discuss the terms of peace. Whether they will be able to come to an agreement or not I can't say. But it is worth while to have obtained the chance of peace, and the only possible way to get this chance was to secure such an agreement of the two powers that they would meet and discuss the terms direct. Of course Japan will want to ask more than she ought to ask, and Russia to give less than she ought to give. Perhaps both sides will prove impracticable. Perhaps one will. But there is the chance that they will prove sensible, and make a peace, which will really be for the interest of each as things are now. At any rate the experiment was worth trying. I have kept the secret very successfully, and my dealings with the Japanese in particular have been known to no one, so that the result is in the nature of a surprise.

QUENTIN'S QUAINT SAYINGS

Oyster Bay, N.Y., Aug. 26, 1905.

DEAR KERMIT:

Mr. Phil Stewart and Dr. Lambert spent a night here, Quentin greeting the former with most cordial friendship, and in explanation stating that he always liked to get acquainted with everybody. I take Hall* to chop, and he plays tennis with Phil and Oliver, and rides with Phil and Quentin. The Plunger (a submarine) has come to the Bay and I am going out in it this afternoon—or rather down on it. N. B.—I have just been down, for 50 minutes; it was very interesting.

Last night I listened to Mother reading "The Lances of Linwood" to the two little boys and then hearing them their prayers. Then I went into Archie's room, where they both showed all their china animals; I read them Laura E. Richards' poems, including "How does the President take his tea?" They christened themselves Punkey Doodle and Jollapin, from the chorus of this, and immediately afterwards I played with them on Archie's bed. First I would toss Punkey Doodle (Quentin) on Jollapin (Archie) and tickle Jollapin while Punkey Doodle squalled and wiggled on top of him, and then reverse them and keep Punkey Doodle down by heaving Jollapin on him, while they both kicked and struggled until my shirt front looked very much the worse for wear. You doubtless remember yourself how bad it was for me, when I was dressed for dinner, to play with all you scamps when you were little.

*Franklyn H. Hall, served the Roosevelt family at Oyster Bay and later as chief messenger at the White House. Ethel and Kermit became godparents of his son, Leonard Wood Hall, later a congressman from New York's 2nd District and national chairman of the Republican party, 1953–1957.

The other day a reporter asked Quentin something about me; to which that affable and canny young gentleman responded, "Yes, I see him sometimes; but I know nothing of his family life."

ADVICE REGARDING NEWSPAPER ANNOYANCES

When Theodore Roosevelt, Jr., entered Harvard as a freshman he had to pay the penalty of being a President's son. Newspaper reporters followed all his movements, especially in athletics, and he was the victim of many exaggerated and often purely fictitious accounts of his doings. His father wrote him indignant and sympathetic letters, two of which are reproduced here.

White House, October 2, 1905.

BLESSED OLD TED:

The thing to do is to go on just as you have evidently been doing, attract as little attention as possible, do not make a fuss about the newspaper men, camera creatures, and idiots generally, letting it be seen that you do not like them and avoid them, but not letting them betray you into any excessive irritation. I believe they will soon drop you, and it is just an unpleasant thing that you will have to live down. Ted, I have had an enormous number of unpleasant things that I have had to live down in my life at different times and you have begun to have them now. I saw that you were not out on the football field on Saturday and was rather glad of it, as evidently those infernal idiots were eagerly waiting for you, but whenever you do go you will have to make up your mind that they will make it exceedingly unpleasant for you for once or twice, and you will just have to bear it; for you can never in the world afford to let them drive you away from anything you intend to do, whether it is football or anything else, and by going about your own business quietly and pleasantly, doing just what you would do if they were not there, generally they will get tired of it, and the boys themselves will see that it is not your fault, and will feel, if anything, rather a sympathy for you. Meanwhile I want you to know that we are all thinking of you and sympathizing with you the whole time; and it is a great comfort to me to have such confidence in you and to know that though these creatures can cause you a little trouble and make you feel a little downcast, they can not drive you one way or the other, or make you alter the course you have set out for yourself.

We were all of us, I am almost ashamed to say, rather blue at getting back in the White House, simply because we missed Sagamore Hill so much. But it is very beautiful and we feel very ungrateful at having even a passing fit of blueness, and we are enjoying it to the full now. I have just seen Archie dragging some fifty foot of hose pipe across the tennis court to play in the sand-box. I have been playing tennis with Mr. Pinchot, who beat me three sets to one, the only deuce-set being the one I won.

This is just an occasion to show the stuff there is in you. Do not let these newspaper creatures and kindred idiots drive you one hair's breadth from the line you had marked out in football or anything else. Avoid any fuss, if possible.

White House, October 11, 1905.

DEAR TED:

I was delighted to find from your last letters that you are evidently having a pretty good time in spite of the newspaper and kodak creatures. I guess that nuisance is now pretty well abated. Every now and then they will do something horrid; but I think you can safely, from now on, ignore them entirely.

I shall be interested to hear how you get on, first of all with your studies, in which you seem to have started well, and next with football. I expected that you would find it hard to compete with the other candidates for the position of end, as they are mostly heavier than you; especially since you went off in weight owing to the excitement of your last weeks of holiday in the summer. Of course the fact that you are comparatively light tells against you and gives you a good deal to overcome; and undoubtedly it was from this standpoint not a good thing that you were unable to lead a quieter life toward the end of your stay at Oyster Bay.

So it is about the polo club. In my day we looked with suspicion upon all freshman societies, and the men who tried to get them up or were prominent in them rarely amounted to much in the class afterwards; and it has happened that I have heard rather unfavorably of the polo club. But it may be mere accident that I have thus heard unfavorably about it, and in thirty years the attitude of the best fellows in college to such a thing as a freshman club may have changed so absolutely that my experience can be of no value. Exercise your own best judgment and form some idea of what the really best fellows in the class think on the subject. Do not make the mistake of thinking that the men who are merely undeveloped are really the best fellows, no matter how pleasant and agreeable they are or how popular. Popularity is a good thing, but it is not something for which to sacrifice studies or athletics or good standing in any way; and sometimes to seek it overmuch is to lose it. I do not mean this as applying to you, but as applying to certain men who still have a great vogue at first in the class, and of whom you will naturally tend to think pretty well.

In all these things I can only advise you in a very general way. You are on the ground. You know the men and the general college sentiment. You have gone in with the serious purpose of doing decently and honorably; of standing well in your studies; of showing that in athletics you mean business up to the extent of your capacity, and of getting the respect and liking of your classmates so far as they can be legitimately obtained. As to the exact methods of carrying out these objects, I must trust to you.

INCIDENTS OF A SOUTHERN TRIP

White House, Nov. 1, 1905.

DEAR KERMIT:

I had a great time in the South, and it was very nice indeed having Mr. John McIlhenny* and Mr. John Greenway† with me. Of course I enjoyed most the three days when Mother was there. But I was so well received and had so many things to say which I was really glad to say, that the whole trip was a success. When I left New Orleans on the little lighthouse tender to go down to the gulf where the big war ship was awaiting me, we had a collision. I was standing up at the time and the shock pitched me forward so that I dove right though the window, taking the glass all out except a jagged rim round the very edge. But I went through so quickly that I received only some minute scratches on my face and hands which, however, bled pretty freely. I was very glad to come up the coast on the squadron of great armored cruisers.

In the gulf the weather was hot and calm, but soon after round-

---

*John Avery McIlhenny, former Rough Rider whom TR appointed civil service commissioner. His family manufactured Tabasco sauce on Avery Island, Louisiana.
†John "Jack" Greenway, former Rough Rider and prominent citizen of Arizona.

ing Florida and heading northward we ran into a gale. Admiral Brownson* is a regular little gamecock and he drove the vessels to their limit. It was great fun to see the huge warcraft pounding steadily into the gale and forging onward through the billows. Some of the waves were so high that the water came green over the flying bridge forward, and some of the officers were thrown down and badly bruised. One of the other ships lost a man overboard, and although we hunted for him an hour and a half we could not get him, and had a boat smashed in the endeavor.

When I got back here I found sister, very interesting about her Eastern trip. She has had a great time, and what is more, she has behaved mighty well under rather trying circumstances. Ethel was a dear, as always, and the two little boys were as cunning as possible. Sister had brought them some very small Japanese fencing armor, which they had of course put on with glee, and were clumsily fencing with wooden two-handed swords. And they had also rigged up in the dark nursery a grewsome man with a pumpkin head, which I was ushered in to see, and in addition to the regular eyes, nose, and saw-tooth mouth, Archie had carved in the back of the pumpkin the words "Pumpkin Giant," the candle inside illuminating it beautifully. Mother was waiting for me at the Navy Yard, looking too pretty for anything, when I arrived. She and I had a ride this afternoon. Of course I am up to my ears in work.

The mornings are lovely now, crisp and fresh; after breakfast Mother and I walk around the grounds accompanied by Skip, and also by Slipper, her bell tinkling loudly. The gardens are pretty dishevelled now, but the flowers that are left are still lovely; even yet some honeysuckle is blooming on the porch.

*Rear Admiral Willard Herbert Brownson, superintendent of the Annapolis Naval Academy, later appointed head of the Bureau of Navigation by TR.

POETS AND PRINCES

White House, November 6, 1905.

DEAR KERMIT:

Just a line, for I really have nothing to say this week. I have caught up with my work. One day we had a rather forlorn little poet and his nice wife in at lunch. They made me feel quite badly by being so grateful at my having mentioned him in what I fear was a very patronizing and, indeed, almost supercilious way, as having written an occasional good poem. I am much struck by Robinson's*

two poems which you sent Mother. What a queer, mystical creature he is! I did not understand one of them—that about the gardens—and I do not know that I like either of them quite as much as some of those in "The Children of the Night." But he certainly has got the real spirit of poetry in him. Whether he can make it come out I am not quite sure.

Prince Louis of Battenberg[†] has been here and I have been very much pleased with him. He is a really good admiral, and in addition he is a well-read and cultivated man and it was charming to talk with him. We had him and his nephew, Prince Alexander, a midshipman, to lunch alone with us, and we really enjoyed having them. At the State dinner he sat between me and Bonaparte,[‡] and I could not help smiling to myself in thinking that here was this British Admiral seated beside the American Secretary of the Navy—the

*Edwin Arlington Robinson, outstanding American poet befriended by Kermit and TR.

[†]Prince Louis Alexander of Battenberg, admiral in the British Navy, who was making a goodwill tour to the United States. Later he adopted the name Mountbatten and was the father of Lord Louis Mountbatten.

[‡]Charles Joseph Bonaparte, secretary of the Navy and later attorney general in TR's cabinet.

American Secretary of the Navy being the grandnephew of Napoleon and the grandson of Jerome, King of Westphalia; while the British Admiral was the grandson of a Hessian general who was the subject of King Jerome and served under Napoleon, and then, by no means creditably, deserted him in the middle of the Battle of Leipsic.

I am off to vote to-night.

NOVELS AND GAMES

White House, November 19, 1905.

DEAR KERMIT:

I sympathize with every word you say in your letter, about Nicholas Nickleby, and about novels generally. Normally I only care for a novel if the ending is good, and I quite agree with you that if the hero has to die he ought to die worthily and nobly, so that our sorrow at the tragedy shall be tempered with the joy and pride one always feels when a man does his duty well and bravely. There is quite enough sorrow and shame and suffering and baseness in real life, and there is no need for meeting it unnecessarily in fiction. As Police Commissioner it was my duty to deal with all kinds of squalid misery and hideous and unspeakable infamy, and I should have been worse than a coward if I had shrunk from doing what was necessary; but there would have been no use whatever in my reading novels detailing all this misery and squalor and crime, or at least in reading them as a steady thing. Now and then there is a powerful but sad story which really is interesting and which really does good; but normally the books which do good and the books which healthy people find interesting are those which are not in the least of the sugar-candy variety, but which, while portraying foulness and suffering when they must be portrayed, yet have a joyous as well as a noble side.

We have had a very mild and open fall. I have played tennis a good deal, the French Ambassador* being now quite a steady playmate, as he and I play about alike; and I have ridden with Mother a great deal. Last Monday when Mother had gone to New York I had Selous,† the great African hunter, to spend the day and night. He is a perfect old dear; just as simple and natural as can be and very interesting. I took him, with Bob Bacon,‡ Gifford Pinchot, Ambassador Meyer§ and Jim Garfield, for a good scramble and climb in the afternoon, and they all came to dinner afterwards. Before we came down to dinner I got him to spend three-quarters of an hour in telling delightfully exciting lion and hyena stories to Ethel, Archie and Quentin. He told them most vividly and so enthralled the little boys that the next evening I had to tell them a large number myself.

To-day is Quentin's birthday and he loved his gifts, perhaps most of all the weest, cunningest live pig you ever saw, presented him by Straus.⸢ Phil Stewart and his wife and boy, Wolcott (who is Archie's age), spent a couple of nights here. One afternoon we had hide-and-go-seek, bringing down Mr. Garfield and the Garfield

---

*Jean Jules Jusserand, French ambassador in Washington from 1902 to 1925.

†Frederick Courteney Selous, famous as a professional big-game hunter, also an explorer, author, and naturalist.

‡Robert Bacon, assistant secretary of state, appointed secretary of state by TR in 1909.

§George von Lengerke Meyer, United States ambassador to Italy and Russia, later appointed postmaster general by TR.

⸢Oscar Solomon Straus, wealthy lawyer and diplomat, secretary of commerce and labor in TR's cabinet.

boys, and Archie turning up with the entire football team, who took a day off for the special purpose. We had obstacle races, hide-and-go-seek, blind-man's buff, and everything else; and there were times when I felt that there was a perfect shoal of small boys bursting in every direction up and down stairs, and through and over every conceivable object.

Mother and I still walk around the grounds every day after breakfast. The gardens, of course, are very, very dishevelled now, the snap-dragons holding out better than any other flowers.

CHRISTMAS PRESENT TO HIS OLD NURSE
(To Mrs. Dora Watkins)

White House, December 19, 1905.

DEAR DOLLY:

I wish you a merry Christmas, and want you to buy whatever you think you would like with the enclosed check for twenty dollars. It is now just forty years since you stopped being my nurse, when I was a little boy of seven, just one year younger than Quentin now is.

I wish you could see the children play here in the White House grounds. For the last three days there has been snow, and Archie and Quentin and their cousin, cunning little Sheffield Cowles, and their other cousin, Mr. John Elliott's little girl, Helena, who is a perfect little dear, have been having all kinds of romps in the snow—coasting, having snowball fights, and doing everything—in the grounds back of the White House. This coming Saturday afternoon I have agreed to have a great play of hide-and-go-seek in the White House itself, not only with these children but with their various small friends.

DICKENS AND THACKERAY

White House, February 3, 1906.

DEAR KERMIT:

I agree pretty well with your views of David Copperfield. Dora was very cunning and attractive, but I am not sure that the husband would retain enough respect for her to make life quite what it ought to be with her. This is a harsh criticism and I have known plenty of women of the Dora type whom I have felt were a good deal better than the men they married, and I have seen them sometimes make very happy homes. I also feel as you do that if a man had to struggle on and make his way it would be a great deal better to have some one like Sophie. Do you recollect that dinner at which David Copperfield and Traddles were, where they are described as seated at the dinner, one "in the glare of the red velvet lady" and the other "in the gloom of Hamlet's aunt"? I am so glad you like Thackeray. "Pendennis" and "The Newcomes" and "Vanity Fair" I can read over and over again.

Ted blew in to-day. I think he has been studying pretty well this term and now he is through all his examinations but one. He hopes, and I do, that you will pay what attention you can to athletics. Play hockey, for instance, and try to get into shape for the mile run. I know it is too short a distance for you, but if you will try for the hare and hounds running and the mile, too, you may be able to try for the two miles when you go to Harvard.

The weather was very mild early in the week. It has turned cold now; but Mother and I had a good ride yesterday, and Ted and I a good ride this afternoon, Ted on Grey Dawn. We have been having a perfect whirl of dinner engagements; but thank heavens they will stop shortly after Sister's wedding.

A TRIBUTE TO ARCHIE

White House, March 11, 1906.

DEAR KERMIT:

I agree pretty much to all your views both about Thackeray and Dickens, although you care for some of Thackeray of which I am not personally fond. Mother loves it all. Mother, by the way, has been reading "The Legend of Montrose" to the little boys and they are absorbed in it. She finds it hard to get anything that will appeal to both Archie and Quentin, as they possess such different natures.

I am quite proud of what Archie did the day before yesterday. Some of the bigger boys were throwing a baseball around outside of Mr. Sidwell's* school and it hit one of them square in the eye, breaking all the blood-vessels and making an extremely dangerous hurt. The other boys were all rattled and could do nothing, finally sneaking off when Mr. Sidwell appeared. Archie stood by and himself promptly suggested that the boy should go to Dr. Wilmer.† Accordingly he scorched down to Dr. Wilmer's and said there was an emergency case for one of Mr. Sidwell's boys, who was hurt in the eye, and could he bring him. Dr. Wilmer, who did not know Archie was there, sent out word to of course do so. So Archie scorched back on his wheel, got the boy (I do not know why Mr. Sidwell did not take him himself) and led him down to Dr. Wilmer's, who attended to his eye and had to send him at once to a hospital, Archie waiting until he heard the result and then coming home. Dr. Wilmer told me about it and said if

*Mr. Thomas Sidwell, principal of the Friends' Select School in Washington.
†Dr. William Holland Wilmer, prominent opthamologist of the Johns Hopkins University.

Archie had not acted with such promptness the boy (who was four or five years older than Archie, by the way) would have lost his sight.

What a heavenly place a sandbox is for two little boys! Archie and Quentin play industriously in it during most of their spare moments when out in the grounds. I often look out of the office windows when I have a score of Senators and Congressmen with me and see them both hard at work arranging caverns or mountains, with runways for their marbles.

Good-bye, blessed fellow. I shall think of you very often during the coming week, and I am so very glad that Mother is to be with you at your confirmation.

PILLOW FIGHTS WITH THE BOYS

White House, March 19, 1906.

DARLING KERMIT:

. . . .

During the four days Mother was away I made a point of seeing the children each evening for three-quarters of an hour or so. Archie and Quentin are really great playmates. One night I came up-stairs and found Quentin playing the pianola as hard as he could, while Archie would suddenly start from the end of the hall where the pianola was, and, accompanied by both the dogs, race as hard as he could the whole length of the White House clean to the other end of the hall and then tear back again. Another evening as I came up-stairs I found Archie and Quentin having a great play, chuckling with laughter, Archie driving Quentin by his suspenders, which were fixed to the end of a pair of woollen reins. Then they would ambush me and we would have a vigorous pillow-fight, and after five or ten minutes of this we would go into Mother's room, and I would read them the book Mother had been reading them, "The Legend of Montrose." We just got through it the very last evening. Both Skip and Jack have welcomed Mother back with frantic joy, and this morning came in and lay on her bed as soon as she had finished breakfast—for she did not come down to either breakfast or lunch, as she is going to spend the night at Baltimore with the Bonapartes.

I was so interested in your reading "Phineas Finn" that I ordered a copy myself. I have also ordered DeQuincey's works, as I find we have not got them at the White House.

. . . .

SORROWS OF SKIP

White House, April 1, 1906.

DARLING ARCHIE:

Poor Skip is a very, very lonely little dog without his family. Each morning he comes up to see me at breakfast time and during most of breakfast (which I take in the hall just outside my room) Skip stands with his little paws on my lap. Then when I get through and sit down in the rocking-chair to read for fifteen or twenty minutes, Skip hops into my lap and stays there, just bathing himself in the companionship of the only one of his family he has left. The rest of the day he spends with the ushers, as I am so frightfully busy that I am nowhere long enough for Skip to have any real satisfaction in my companionship. Poor Jack has never come home. We may never know what became of him.

"AN INTERESTING CIRCUS EXPERIENCE"

White House, April 1, 1906.

DARLING ETHEL:

I haven't heard a word from the two new horses, and I rather believe that if there had been any marked improvement in either of them I should have heard. I gather that one at least and probably both would be all right for me if I were twenty years younger, and would probably be all right for Ted now; but of course as things are at present I do not want a horse with which I have an interesting circus experience whenever we meet an automobile, or one which I cannot get to go in any particular direction without devoting an hour or two to the job. So that it looks as if old Rusty would be good enough for me for some time to come. I am going out on him with Senator Lodge this afternoon, and he will be all right and as fresh as paint, for he has been three days in the stable. But to-day is just a glorious spring day—March having ended as it began, with rain and snow—and I will have a good ride. I miss Mother and you children very much, of course, but I believe you are having a good time, and I am really glad you are to see Havana.

A BIG AND LONELY WHITE HOUSE

White House, April 1, 1906.

DARLING QUENTY-QUEE:

Slipper and the kittens are doing finely. I think the kittens will be big enough for you to pet and have some satisfaction out of when you get home, although they will be pretty young still. I miss you all dreadfully, and the house feels big and lonely and full of echoes with nobody but me in it; and I do not hear any small scamps running up and down the hall just as hard as they can; or hear their voices while I am dressing; or suddenly look out through the windows of the office at the tennis ground and see them racing over it or playing in the sand-box. I love you very much.

A NEW PUPPY AND A NEW HORSE

White House, April 12, 1906.

DEAR KERMIT:

. . . .

Last night I played "tickley" in their room with the two little boys. As we rolled and bounced over all three beds in the course of the play, not to mention frantic chases under them, I think poor Mademoiselle was rather appalled at the result when we had finished. Archie's seven-weeks-old St. Bernard puppy has come and it is the dearest puppy imaginable; a huge, soft thing, which Archie carries around in his arms and which the whole family love.

Yesterday I took a first ride on the new horse, Roswell, Captain Lee* going along on Rusty as a kind of a nurse. Roswell is not yet four and he is really a green colt and not quite the horse I want at present, as I haven't time to fuss with him, and am afraid of letting the Sergeant ride him, as he does not get on well with him, and there is nobody else in our stable that can ride at all. He is a beautiful horse, a wonderful jumper, and does not pull at all. He shies pretty badly, especially when he meets an automobile; and when he

---

*Fitzhugh Lee, captain in the United States Army and aide to TR.

leaves the stable or strikes a road that he thinks will take him home and is not allowed to go down it, he is apt to rear, which I do not like; but I am inclined to think that he will get over these traits, and if I can arrange to have Lee handle him a couple of months more, and if Ted and I can regularly ride him down at Oyster Bay, I think that he will turn out all right.

Mother and I walk every morning through the grounds, which, of course, are lovely. Not only are the song-sparrows and robins singing, but the white-throated sparrows, who will, I suppose, soon leave us for the North, are still in full song, and this morning they waked us up at daybreak singing just outside the window.

A QUENTIN ANECDOTE

White House, April 22, 1906.

DEAR KERMIT:

Ted has been as good and cunning as possible. He has completely recovered from the effects of having his eye operated upon, and though the eye itself is a somewhat gruesome object, Ted is in the highest spirits. He goes back to Harvard to-day.

. . . .

As I write, Archie and Quentin are busily engaged in the sand-box and I look out across the tennis-ground at them. If ever there was a heaven-sent treasure to small boys, that sand-box is the treasure. It was very cunning to see the delight various little children took in it at the egg-rolling on Easter Monday. Thanks to our decision in keeping out grown people and stopping everything at one o'clock, the egg-rolling really was a children's festival, and was pretty and not objectionable this year.

The apple trees are now coming into bloom, including that big arched apple tree, under which Mother and I sit, by the fountain, on the stone bench. It is the apple tree that Mother particularly likes. . . .

Did Quentin write his poems after you had gone? I never can recollect whether you have seen them or not. He is a funny small person if ever there was one. The other day we were discussing a really dreadful accident which had happened; a Georgetown young man having taken out a young girl in a canoe on the river, the canoe upset and the girl was drowned; whereupon the young man, when he got home, took what seemed to us an exceedingly cold-blooded method of a special delivery letter to notify her parents. We were expressing our horror at his sending a special delivery letter, and Quentin solemnly chimed in with "Yes, he wasted ten cents." There was a moment's eloquent silence, and then we strove to explain to Quentin that what we were objecting to was not in the least the young man's spendthrift attitude!

As I walk to and from the office now the terrace is fairly fragrant with the scent of the many-colored hyacinths which Mother has put out in boxes on the low stone walls.

. . . .

A VISIT TO WASHINGTON'S BIRTHPLACE

White House, April 30, 1906.

DEAR KERMIT:

On Saturday afternoon Mother and I started off on the *Sylph*, Mother having made up her mind I needed thirty-six hours' rest, and we had a delightful time together, and she was just as cunning as she could be. On Sunday Mother and I spent about four hours ashore, taking our lunch and walking up to the monument which marks where the house stood in which Washington was born. It is a simple shaft. Every vestige of the house is destroyed, but a curious and rather pathetic thing is that, although it must be a hundred years since the place was deserted, there are still multitudes of flowers which must have come from those in the old garden. There are iris and narcissus and a little blue flower, with a neat, prim, clean smell that makes one feel as if it ought to be put with lavender into chests of fresh old linen. The narcissus in particular was growing around everywhere, together with real wild flowers like the painted columbine and star of Bethlehem. It was a lovely spot on a headland overlooking a broad inlet from the Potomac. There was also the old graveyard or grave plot in which were the gravestones of Washington's father and mother and grandmother, all pretty nearly ruined. It was lovely warm weather and Mother and I enjoyed our walk through the funny lonely old country. Mocking-birds, meadow-larks, Carolina wrens, cardinals, and field sparrows were singing cheerfully. We came up the river in time to get home last evening. This morning Mother and I walked around the White House grounds as usual. I think I get more fond of flowers every year. The grounds are now at that high stage of beauty in which they will stay for the next two months. The buckeyes are in bloom, the pink dogwood, and the fragrant lilacs, which are almost the loveliest of the bushes; and then the flowers, including the lily-of-the-valley.

I am dictating in the office. Archie is out by the sandbox playing with the hose. The playing consists in brandishing it around his head and trying to escape the falling water. He escapes about twice out of three times and must now be a perfect drowned rat. (I have just had him in to look at him and he is even more of a drowned rat than I supposed. He has gone out to complete his shower bath under strict promise that immediately afterwards he will go in and change his clothes.)

Quentin is the funniest mite you ever saw and certainly a very original little fellow. He left at Mademoiselle's plate yesterday a large bunch of flowers with the inscription that they were from the fairies to her to reward her for taking care of "two *good, good* boys." Ethel is a dear.

MORE ABOUT DICKENS

White House, May 20, 1906.

DEAR TED:

Mother read us your note and I was interested in the discussion between you and ————* over Dickens. Dickens' characters are really to a great extent personified attributes rather than individuals. In consequence, while there are not nearly as many who are actually like people one meets, as for instance in Thackeray, there are a great many more who possess *characteristics* which we encounter continually, though rarely as strongly developed as in the fictional originals. So Dickens' characters last almost as Bunyan's do. For instance, Jefferson Brick and Elijah Pogram and Hannibal Chollop are all real personifications of certain bad tendencies in American life, and I am continually thinking of or alluding to some newspaper editor or Senator or homicidal rowdy by one of these three names. I never met any one exactly like Uriah Heep,

---

*This name was obliterated by an inkblot in the original letter to Ted and thus left blank by TR's editor.

but now and then we see individuals show traits which make it easy to describe them, with reference to those traits, as Uriah Heep. It is just the same with Micawber. Mrs. Nickleby is not quite a real person, but she typifies, in accentuated form, traits which a great many real persons possess, and I am continually thinking of her when I meet them. There are half a dozen books of Dickens which have, I think, furnished more characters which are the constant companions of the ordinary educated man around us, than is true of any other half-dozen volumes published within the same period.

NO PLACE LIKE SAGAMORE HILL
(To Ethel, at Sagamore Hill)

White House, June 11, 1906.

BLESSED ETHEL:

I am very glad that what changes have been made in the house are good, and I look forward so eagerly to seeing them. After all, fond as I am of the White House and much though I have appreciated these years in it, there isn't any place in the world like home—like Sagamore Hill, where things are our own, with our own associations, and where it is real country.

ATTIC DELIGHTS

White House, June 17, 1906.

BLESSED ETHEL:

Your letter delighted me. I read it over twice, and chuckled over it. By George, how entirely I sympathize with your feelings in the attic!

I know just what it is to get up into such a place and find the delightful, winding passages where one lay hidden with thrills of criminal delight, when the grownups were vainly demanding one's appearance at some legitimate and abhorred function; and then the once-beloved and half-forgotten treasures, and the emotions of peace and war, with reference to former companions, which they recall.

I am not in the least surprised about the mental telepathy; there is much in it and in kindred things which are real and which at present we do not understand. The only trouble is that it usually gets mixed up with all kinds of fakes.

I am glad the band had a healthy effect in reviving old Bleistein's youth. I shall never forget the intense interest in life he always used to gain when we encountered an Italian with a barrel organ and a bear—a combination that made Renown seek instant refuge in attempted suicide.

I am really pleased that you are going to teach Sunday school. I think I told you that I taught it for seven years, most of the time in a mission class, my pupils being of a kind which furnished me plenty of vigorous excitement.

PRESIDENTIAL RESCUE OF A KITTEN

White House, June 24, 1906.

DARLING ETHEL:

To-day as I was marching to church, with Sloan* some 25 yards behind, I suddenly saw two terriers racing to attack a kitten which

*Jimmie Sloan, a Secret Service man at the White House.

was walking down the sidewalk. I bounced forward with my umbrella, and after some active work put to flight the dogs while Sloan captured the kitten, which was a friendly, helpless little thing, evidently too well accustomed to being taken care of to know how to shift for itself. I inquired of all the bystanders and of people on the neighboring porches to know if they knew who owned it; but as they all disclaimed, with many grins, any knowledge of it, I marched ahead with it in my arms for about half a block. Then I saw a very nice colored woman and little colored girl looking out of the window of a small house with on the door a dressmaker's advertisement, and I turned and walked up the steps and asked if they did not want the kitten. They said they did, and the little girl welcomed it lovingly; so I felt I had gotten it a home and continued toward church.

Has the lordly Ted turned up yet? Is his loving sister able, unassisted, to reduce the size of his head, or does she need any assistance from her male parent?

Your affectionate father,

The Tyrant.

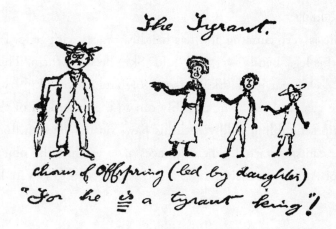

chorus of Offspring (led by daughter)
"For he is a tyrant king"!

SPORTS OF QUENTIN AND ARCHIE

Oyster Bay, Aug. 18, 1906.

DEAR KERMIT:

. . . .

Quentin is the same cheerful pagan philosopher as ever. He swims like a little duck; rides well; stands quite severe injuries without complaint, and is really becoming a manly little fellow. Archie is devoted to the *Why* (sailboat). The other day while Mother and I were coming in, rowing, we met him sailing out, and it was too cunning for anything. The *Why* looks exactly like a little black wooden shoe with a sail in it, and the crew consisted of Archie, of one of his beloved playmates, a seaman from the *Sylph*, and of Skip—very alert and knowing.

SKIP AND ARCHIE

White House, October 23, 1906.

DEAR KERMIT:

Archie is very cunning and has handicap races with Skip. He spreads his legs, bends over, and holds Skip between them. Then he says, "On your mark, Skip, ready; go!" and shoves Skip back while he runs as hard as he possibly can to the other end of the hall, Skip scrambling wildly with his paws on the smooth floor until he can get started, when he races after Archie, the object being for Archie to reach the other end before Skip can overtake him.

A TURKEY HUNT AT PINE KNOT

White House, November 4, 1906.

DEAR KERMIT:

Just a line to tell you what a nice time we had at Pine Knot. Mother was as happy as she always is there, and as cunning and pretty as possible. As for me, I hunted faithfully through all three days, leaving the house at three o'clock one day, at four the next, and at five the next, so that I began my hunts in absolute night; but fortunately we had a brilliant moon on each occasion. The first two days were failures. I did not see a turkey, and on each occasion when everybody was perfectly certain that I was going to see a turkey, something went wrong and the turkey did not turn up. The last day I was out thirteen hours, and you may imagine how hungry I was when I got back, not to speak of being tired; though fortunately most of the time I was rambling around on horseback, so I was not done out. But in the afternoon at last luck changed, and then for once everything went right. The hunter who was with me marked a turkey in a point of pines stretching down from a forest into an open valley, with another forest on its farther side. I ran down to the end of the point and hid behind a bush. He walked down through the pines and the turkey came out and started to fly across the valley, offering me a beautiful side shot at about thirty-five yards—just the distance for my ten-bore. I killed it dead, and felt mighty happy as it came tumbling down through the air.

⌒

In November, 1906, the President, accompanied by Mrs. Roosevelt, went to the Isthmus of Panama, where he spent three days in inspecting the work of building the Panama Canal, returning by way of Porto Rico. The journey was taken on the naval vessel Louisiana, *and many of his letters to the children were written while on board that vessel and mailed after reaching Colon.*

PETS ON SHIPBOARD

On Board U.S.S. *Louisiana,* On the Way to Panama. Sunday, November 11, 1906.

BLESSED QUENTIN:

You would be amused at the pets they have aboard this ship. They have two young bull-dogs, a cat, three little raccoons, and a tiny Cuban goat. They seem to be very amicable with one another, although I think the cat has suspicions of all the rest. The coons clamber about everywhere, and the other afternoon while I was sitting reading, I suddenly felt my finger seized in a pair of soft black paws and found the coon sniffing at it, making me feel a little uncomfortable lest it might think the finger something good to eat. The two puppies play endlessly. One of them belongs to Lieutenant Evans. The crew will not be allowed ashore at Panama or else I know they would pick up a whole raft of other pets there. The jackies seem especially fond of the little coons. A few minutes ago I saw one of the jackies strolling about with a coon perched upon his shoulder, and now and then he would reach up his hand and give it a small piece of bread to eat.

NAMES OF THE GUNS

On Board U.S.S. *Louisiana*, Sunday, November 11, 1906.

BLESSED ARCHIE:

I wish you were along with us, for you would thoroughly enjoy everything on this ship. We have had three days of perfect weather, while this great battleship with her two convoys, the great armored cruisers, *Tennessee* and *Washington*, have steamed steadily in column ahead southward through calm seas until now we are in the tropics. They are three as splendid ships of their class as there are afloat, save only the English Dreadnaught. The *Louisiana* now has her gun-sights and everything is all in good shape for her to begin the practice of the duties which will make her crew as fit for man-of-war's work as the crew of any one of our other first-class battleships. The men are such splendid-looking fellows, Americans of the best type, young, active, vigorous, with lots of intelligence. I was much amused at the names of the seven-inch guns, which include *Victor*, *Invincible*, *Peacemaker*, together with *Skidoo*, and also one called *Tedd* and one called *The Big Stick*.

REFLECTIONS ON THE WAY

On Board U.S.S. *Louisiana*, Nov. 13.

DEAR KERMIT:

So far this trip has been a great success, and I think Mother has really enjoyed it. As for me, I of course feel a little bored, as I always do on shipboard, but I have brought on a great variety of books, and am at this moment reading Milton's prose works, "Tacitus," and a German novel called "Jorn Uhl." Mother and I walk briskly up and down the deck together, or else sit aft under the awning, or in the after cabin, with the gun ports open, and read; and I also spend a good deal of time on the forward bridge, and sometimes on the aft bridge, and of course have gone over the ship to inspect it with the Captain. It is a splendid thing to see one of these men-of-war, and it does really make one proud of one's country. Both the officers and the enlisted men are as fine a set as one could wish to see.

It is a beautiful sight, these three great warships standing southward in close column, and almost as beautiful at night when we see not only the lights but the loom through the darkness of the ships astern. We are now in the tropics and I have thought a good deal of the time over eight years ago when I was sailing to Santiago in the fleet of warships and transports. It seems a strange thing to think of my now being President, going to visit the work of the Panama Canal which I have made possible.

Mother, very pretty and dainty in white summer clothes, came up on Sunday morning to see inspection and review, or whatever they call it, of the men. I usually spend half an hour on deck before Mother is dressed. Then we breakfast together alone; have also taken lunch alone, but at dinner have two or three officers to dine with us. Doctor Rixey is along, and is a perfect dear, as always.

EVENTS SINCE COLUMBUS'S DISCOVERY

November 14th.

The fourth day out was in some respects the most interesting. All the forenoon we had Cuba on our right and most of the forenoon and part of the afternoon Hayti on our left; and in each case green, jungly shores and bold mountains—two great, beautiful, venomous tropic islands. These are historic seas and Mother and I have kept thinking of all that has happened in them since Columbus landed at San Salvador (which we also saw), the Spanish explorers, the buccaneers, the English and Dutch sea-dogs and adventurers, the great English and French fleets, the desperate fighting, the triumphs, the pestilences, of all the turbulence, the splendor and the wickedness, and the hot, evil, riotous life of the old planters and slave-owners, Spanish, French, English, and Dutch;—their extermination of the Indians, and bringing in of negro slaves, the decay of most of the islands, the turning of Hayti into a land of savage negroes, who have reverted to voodooism and cannibalism; the effort we are now making to bring Cuba and Porto Rico forward.

To-day is calm and beautiful, as all the days have been on our trip. We have just sighted the highest land of Panama ahead of us, and we shall be at anchor by two o'clock this afternoon; just a little less than six days from the time we left Washington.

PRIDE IN AMERICA

On Board U.S.S. *Louisiana,* Nov. 14.

DEAR TED:

I am very glad to have taken this trip, although as usual I am bored by the sea. Everything has been smooth as possible, and it has been lovely having Mother along. It gives me great pride in America to be aboard this great battleship and to see not only the material perfection of the ship herself in engines, guns and all arrangements, but the fine quality of the officers and crew. Have you ever read Smollett's novel, I think "Roderick Random" or "Humphrey Clinker," in which the hero goes to sea? It gives me an awful idea of what a floating hell of filth, disease, tyranny, and cruelty a war-ship was in those days. Now every arrangement is as clean and healthful as possible. The men can bathe and do bathe as often as cleanliness requires. Their fare is excellent and they are as self-respecting a set as can be imagined. I am no great believer in the superiority of times past; and I have no question that the officers and men of our Navy now are in point of fighting capacity better than in the times of Drake and Nelson; and morally and in physical surroundings the advantage is infinitely in our favor.

It was delightful to have you two or three days at Washington. Blessed old fellow, you had a pretty hard time in college this fall; but it can't be helped, Ted; as one grows older the bitter and the sweet keep coming together. The only thing to do is to grin and bear it, to flinch as little as possible under the punishment, and to keep pegging steadily away until the luck turns.

WHAT THE PRESIDENT SAW AT PANAMA

U.S.S. *Louisiana*, At Sea, November 20, 1906.

DEAR KERMIT:

Our visit to Panama was most successful as well as most interesting. We were there three days and we worked from morning till night. The second day I was up at a quarter to six and got to bed at a quarter of twelve, and I do not believe that in the intervening time, save when I was dressing, there were ten consecutive minutes when I was not busily at work in some shape or form. For two days there [were] uninterrupted tropic rains without a glimpse of the sun, and the Chagres River rose in a flood, higher than any for fifteen years; so that we saw the climate at its worst. It was just what I desired to do.

It certainly adds to one's pleasure to have read history and to appreciate the picturesque. When on Wednesday we approached the coast, and the jungle-covered mountains looked clearer and clearer until we could see the surf beating on the shores, while there was hardly a sign of human habitation, I kept thinking of the four centuries of wild and bloody romance, mixed with abject squalor and suffering, which had made up the history of the Isthmus until three years ago. I could see Balboa crossing at Darien, and the wars between the Spaniards and the Indians, and the settlement and the building up of the quaint walled Spanish towns; and the trade, across the seas by galleon, and over land by pack-train and river canoe, in gold and silver, in precious stones; and then the advent of the buccaneers, and of the English seamen, of Drake and Frobisher and Morgan, and many, many others, and the wild destruction they wrought. Then I thought of the rebellion against the Spanish dominion, and the uninterrupted and bloody wars that followed, the last occurring when I became President; wars, the victorious heroes of which have their pictures frescoed on the quaint rooms of the palace at Panama city, and in similar palaces in all capitals of these strange, turbulent little half-caste civilizations. Meanwhile the Panama railroad had been built by Americans over a half century ago, with appalling loss of life, so that it is said, of course with exaggeration, that every sleeper laid represented the death of a man. Then the French canal company started work, and for two or three years did a good deal, until it became evident that the task far exceeded its powers; and then to miscalculation and inefficiency was added the hideous greed of adventurers, trying each to save something from the general wreck, and the company closed with infamy and scandal.

Now we have taken hold of the job. We have difficulties with our own people, of course. I haven't a doubt that it will take a little longer and cost a little more than men now appreciate, but I believe that the work is being done with a very high degree both of efficiency and honesty; and I am immensely struck by the character of American employees who are engaged, not merely in superintending the work, but in doing all the jobs that need skill and intelligence. The steam shovels, the dirt trains, the machine shops, and the like, are all filled with American engineers, conductors, machinists, boiler-makers, carpenters. From the top to the bottom these men are so hardy, so efficient, so energetic, that it is a real pleasure to look at them. Stevens,* the head engineer, is a big fellow, a man of daring and good sense, and burly power. All of these men are quite as formidable, and would, if it were necessary, do quite as much in battle as the crews of Drake and Morgan; but as it is, they are doing a work of infinitely more lasting consequence. Nothing whatever remains to show what Drake and Morgan did. They produced no real effect down here, but Stevens and his men are changing the face of the continent, are doing the greatest engineering feat of the ages, and the effect of their work will be felt while our civilization lasts. I went over everything that I could possibly go over in the time at my disposal. I examined the quarters of married and single men, white men and negroes. I went over the ground of the Gatun and La Boca dams; went through Panama and Colon, and spent a day in the Culebra cut, where the great work is being done. There the huge steam-shovels are hard at it; scooping huge masses of rock and gravel and dirt previously loosened by the drillers and dynamite blasters, loading it on trains which take it away to some dump, either in the jungle or where the dams are to be built. They are eating steadily into the mountain, cutting it down

---

*John F. Stevens, chief engineer of the Panama Canal operation 1905–1907, later chairman of the Isthmian Canal Commission.

and down. Little tracks are laid on the side-hills, rocks blasted out, and the great ninety-five ton steam-shovels work up like mountain howitzers until they come to where they can with advantage begin their work of eating into and destroying the mountainside. With intense energy men and machines do their task, the white men supervising matters and handling the machines, while the tens of thousands of black men do the rough manual labor where it is not worth while to have machines do it. It is an epic feat, and one of immense significance.

The deluge of rain meant that many of the villages were knee-deep in water, while the flooded rivers tore through the tropic forests. It is a real tropic forest, palms and bananas, breadfruit trees, bamboos, lofty ceibas, and gorgeous butterflies and brilliant colored birds fluttering among the orchids. There are beautiful flowers too.

All my old enthusiasm for natural history seemed to revive, and I would have given a good deal to have stayed and tried to collect specimens. It would be a good hunting country too; deer, and now and then jaguars and tapir, and great birds that they call wild turkeys; there are alligators in the rivers. One of the trained nurses from the hospital went to bathe in a pool last August and an alligator grabbed him by the legs and was making off with him, but was fortunately scared away, leaving the man badly injured.

I tramped everywhere through the mud. Mother did not do the roughest work, and had time to see more of the really picturesque and beautiful side of the life, and really enjoyed herself.

P.S. The Gatun dam will make a lake miles long, and the railroad now goes on what will be the bottom of this lake, and it was curious to think that in a few years great ships would be floating in water 100 feet above where we were.

ON THE WAY TO PORTO RICO

U.S.S. *Louisiana*, At Sea, November 20, 1906.

DEAR TED:

This is the third day out from Panama. We have been steaming steadily in the teeth of the trade wind. It has blown pretty hard, and the ship has pitched a little, but not enough to make either Mother or me uncomfortable.

Panama was a great sight. In the first place it was strange and beautiful with its mass of luxuriant tropic jungle, with the treacherous tropic rivers trailing here and there through it; and it was lovely to see the orchids and brilliant butterflies and the strange birds and snakes and lizards, and finally the strange old Spanish towns and the queer thatch and bamboo huts of the ordinary natives. In the next place it is a tremendous sight to see the work on the canal going on. From the chief engineer and the chief sanitary officer down to the last arrived machinist or time-keeper, the five thousand Americans at work on the Isthmus seemed to me an exceptionally able, energetic lot, some of them grumbling, of course, but on the whole a mighty good lot of men. The West Indian negroes offer a greater problem, but they are doing pretty well also. I was astonished at the progress made. We spent the three days in working from dawn until long after darkness—dear Dr. Rixey being, of course, my faithful companion. Mother would see all she liked and then would go off on a little spree by herself, and she enjoyed it to the full.

WHAT HE SAW IN PORTO RICO

U.S.S. *Louisiana*, At Sea, November 23, 1906.

DEAR KERMIT:

We had a most interesting two days at Porto Rico. We landed on the south side of the island and were received by the Governor and the rest of the administration, including nice Mr. Lawrence Grahame;* then were given a reception by the Alcalde and people of Ponce; and then went straight across the island in automobiles to San Juan on the north shore. It was an eighty mile trip and really delightful. The road wound up to the high mountains of the middle island, through them, and then down again to the flat plain on the north shore. The scenery was beautiful. It was as thoroughly tropical as Panama but much more livable. There were palms, tree-ferns, bananas, mangoes, bamboos, and many other trees and multitudes of brilliant flowers. There was one vine called the dream-vine with flowers as big as great white water-lilies, which close up tight in the day-time and bloom at night. There were vines with masses of brilliant purple and pink flowers, and others with masses of little white flowers, which at night-time smell deliciously. There were trees studded over with huge white flowers, and others, the flamboyants such as I saw in the campaign at Santiago, are a mass of large scarlet blossoms in June, but which now had shed them. I thought the tree-ferns especially beautiful. The towns were just such as you saw in Cuba, quaint, brilliantly colored, with the old church or cathedral fronting the plaza, and the plaza always full of flowers. Of course the towns are dirty, but they are not nearly as dirty and offensive as those of Italy; and there is

---

*Lawrence Hill Grahame, commissioner of the interior in Puerto Rico.

something pathetic and childlike about the people. We are giving them a good government and the island is prospering. I never saw a finer set of young fellows than those engaged in the administration. Mr. Grahame, whom of course you remember, is the intimate friend and ally of the leaders of the administration, that is of Governor Beekman Winthrop and of the Secretary of State, Mr. Regis Post. Grahame is a perfect trump and such a handsome, athletic fellow, and a real Sir Galahad. Any wrong-doing, and especially any cruelty makes him flame with fearless indignation. He perfectly delighted the Porto Ricans and also immensely puzzled them by coming in his Scotch kilt to a Government ball. Accordingly, at my special request, I had him wear his kilt at the state dinner and reception the night we were at the palace. You know he is a descendant of Montrose, and although born in Canada, his parents were Scotch and he was educated in Scotland. Do tell Mr. Bob Fergie about him and his kilts when you next write him.

We spent the night at the palace, which is half palace and half castle, and was the residence of the old Spanish governors. It is nearly four hundred years old, and is a delightful building, with quaint gardens and a quaint sea-wall looking over the bay. There were colored lanterns lighting up the gardens for the reception, and the view across the bay in the moonlight was lovely. Our rooms were as attractive as possible too, except that they were so very airy and open that we found it difficult to sleep—not that that much mattered as, thanks to the earliness of our start and the lateness of our reception, we had barely four hours in which we even tried to sleep.

The next morning we came back in automobiles over different and even more beautiful roads. The mountain passes through and over which we went made us feel as if we were in a tropic Switzerland. We had to cross two or three rivers where big cream-colored oxen with yokes tied to their horns pulled the automobiles through the water. At one funny little village we had an open air lunch, very good, of chicken and eggs and bread, and some wine contributed by a wealthy young Spaniard who rode up from a neighboring coffee ranch.

Yesterday afternoon we embarked again, and that evening the crew gave a theatrical entertainment on the afterdeck, closing with three boxing bouts. I send you the program. It was great fun, the audience being equally enraptured with the sentimental songs about the flag, and the sailor's true love and his mother, and with the jokes (the most relished of which related to the fact that bed-bugs were supposed to be so large that they had to be shot!) and the skits about the commissary and various persons and deeds on the ship. In a way the freedom of comment reminded me a little of the Roman triumphs, when the excellent legendaries recited in verse and prose, anything they chose concerning the hero in whose deeds they had shared and whose triumphs they were celebrating. The stage, well lighted, was built on the aftermost part of the deck. We sat in front with the officers, and the sailors behind us in masses on the deck, on the aftermost turrets, on the bridge, and even in the fighting top of the aftermost mast. It was interesting to see their faces in the light.

. . . .

P.S. I forgot to tell you about the banners and inscriptions of welcome to me in Porto Rico. One of them which stretched across the road had on it "Welcome to Theodore and Mrs. Roosevelt." Last evening I really enjoyed a rather funny experience. There is an Army and Navy Union composed chiefly of enlisted men, but also of many officers, and they suddenly held a "garrison" meeting in the torpedo-room of this ship. There were about fifty enlisted men together with the Captain and myself. I was introduced as "comrade and shipmate

Theodore Roosevelt, President of the United States." They were such a nice set of fellows, and I was really so pleased to be with them; so self-respecting, so earnest, and just the right type out of which to make the typical American fighting man who is also a good citizen. The meeting reminded me a good deal of a lodge meeting at Oyster Bay; and of course those men are fundamentally of the same type as the shipwrights, railroad men and fishermen whom I met at the lodge, and who, by the way, are my chief backers politically and are the men who make up the real strength of this nation.

SICKNESS OF ARCHIE

White House, March 3, 1907.

DEAR KERMIT:

Poor little Archie has diphtheria, and we have had a wearing forty-eight hours. Of course it is harder upon Mother a good deal than upon me, because she spends her whole time with him together with the trained nurse, while I simply must attend to my work during these closing hours of Congress (I have worked each day steadily up to half past seven and also in the evening); and only see Archiekins for twenty minutes or a half hour before dinner. The poor little fellow likes to have me put my hands on his forehead, for he says they smell so clean and soapy! Last night he was very sick, but this morning he is better, and Dr. Rixey thinks everything is going well. Dr. Lambert is coming on this afternoon to see him. Ethel, who is away at Philadelphia, will be sent to stay with the Rixeys. Quentin, who has been exposed somewhat to infection, is not allowed to see other little boys, and is leading a career of splendid isolation among the ushers and policemen.

Since I got back here I have not done a thing except work as the President must during the closing days of a session of Congress. Mother was, fortunately, getting much better, but now of course is having a very hard time of it nursing darling little Archie. He is just as good as gold—so patient and loving. Yesterday that scamp Quentin said to Mademoiselle: "If only I had *Archie's* nature, and *my* head, wouldn't it be great?"

In all his sickness Archie remembered that today was Mademoiselle's birthday, and sent her his love and congratulations—which promptly reduced good Mademoiselle to tears.

AT THE JAMESTOWN EXPOSITION

White House, April 29, 1907.

DEAREST KERMIT:

We really had an enjoyable trip to Jamestown. The guests were Mother's friend, Mrs. Johnson, a Virginia lady who reminds me so much of Aunt Annie, my mother's sister, who throughout my childhood was almost as much associated in our home life as my mother herself; Justice Moody, who was as delightful as he always is, and with whom it was a real pleasure to again have a chance to talk; Mr. and Mrs. Bob Bacon, who proved the very nicest guests of all and were companionable and sympathetic at every point. Ethel was as good as gold and took much off of Mother's shoulders in the way of taking care of Quentin. Archie and Quentin had, of course, a heavenly time; went everywhere, below and aloft, and ate indifferently at all hours, both with the officers and enlisted men. We left here Thursday afternoon, and on Friday morning passed in review through the foreign fleet and our own fleet of sixteen great battleships in addition to cruisers. It was an inspiring sight and one I would not have missed for a great deal. Then we went in a launch to the Exposition where I had the usual experience in such cases, made the usual speech, held the usual reception, went to the usual lunch, etc., etc.

In the evening Mother and I got on the *Sylph* and went to Norfolk to dine. When the *Sylph* landed we were met by General Grant* to convoy us to the house. I was finishing dressing, and Mother went out into the cabin and sat down to receive him. In a minute or two I came out and began to hunt for my hat. Mother sat very erect and pretty, looking at my efforts with a tolerance that gradually changed to impatience. Finally she arose to get her own cloak, and then I found that she had been sitting gracefully but firmly on the hat herself—it was a crush hat and it had been flattened until it looked like a wrinkled pie. Mother did not see what she had done so I speechlessly thrust the hat toward her; but she still did not understand and took it as an inexplicable jest of mine merely saying, "Yes, dear," and with patient dignity, turned and went out of the door with General Grant.

The next morning we went on the *Sylph* up the James River, and on the return trip visited three of the dearest places you can imagine, Shirley, Westover, and Brandon. I do not know whether I loved most the places themselves or the quaint out-of-the-world Virginia gentlewomen in them. The houses, the grounds, the owners, all were too dear for anything and we loved them. That night we went back to the *Mayflower* and returned here yesterday, Sunday, afternoon.

To-day spring weather seems really to have begun, and after

---

*Major General Frederick Dent Grant, son of General Ulysses S. Grant, commanded the Department of the East.

lunch Mother and I sat under the apple-tree by the fountain. A purple finch was singing in the apple-tree overhead, and the white petals of the blossoms were silently falling. This afternoon Mother and I are going out riding with Senator Lodge.

GENERAL KUROKI

White House, May 12, 1907.

DEAR KERMIT:

. . . .

General Kuroki* and his suite are here and dined with us at a formal dinner last evening. Everything that he says has to be translated, but nevertheless I had a really interesting talk with him, because I am pretty well acquainted with his campaigns. He impressed me much, as indeed all Japanese military and naval officers do. They are a formidable outfit. I want to try to keep on the best possible terms with Japan and never do her any wrong; but I want still more to see our navy maintained at the highest point of efficiency, for it is the real keeper of the peace.

TEMPORARY ABSENCE OF SKIP

The other day Pete got into a most fearful fight and was dreadfully bitten. He was a very forlorn dog indeed when he came home. And on that particular day Skip disappeared and had not turned up when we went to bed. Poor Archie was very uneasy lest Skip should have gone the way of Jack; and Mother and I shared his uneasiness.

*Count Tamesada Kuroki, outstanding general in the Russo-Japanese War.

But about two in the morning we both of us heard a sharp little bark down-stairs and knew it was Skip, anxious to be let in. So down I went and opened the door on the portico, and Skip simply scuttled in and up to Archie's room, where Archie waked up enough to receive him literally with open arms and then went to sleep cuddled up to him.

DEATH OF SKIP

Sagamore Hill, Sept. 21, 1907.

BLESSED ARCHIEKINS:

We felt dreadfully homesick as you and Kermit drove away; when we pass along the bay front we always think of the dory; and we mourn dear little Skip, although perhaps it was as well the little doggie should pass painlessly away, after his happy little life; for the little fellow would have pined for you.

Your letter was a great comfort; we'll send on the football suit and hope you'll enjoy the football. Of course it will all be new and rather hard at first.

The house is "put up"; everything wrapped in white that can be, and all the rugs off the floors. Quentin is reduced to the secret service men for steady companionship.

QUENTIN'S SNAKE ADVENTURE

White House, Sept. 28, 1907.

DEAREST ARCHIE:

Before we left Oyster Bay Quentin had collected two snakes.

He lost one, which did not turn up again until an hour before departure, when he found it in one of the spare rooms. This one he left loose, and brought the other one to Washington, there being a variety of exciting adventures on the way; the snake wriggling out of his box once, and being upset on the floor once. The first day home Quentin was allowed not to go to school but to go about and renew all his friendships. Among other places that he visited was Schmid's animal store, where he left his little snake. Schmid presented him with three snakes, simply to pass the day with—a large and beautiful and very friendly king snake and two little wee snakes. Quentin came hurrying back on his roller skates and burst into the room to show me his treasures. I was discussing certain matters with the Attorney-General at the time, and the snakes were eagerly deposited in my lap. The king snake, by the way, although most friendly with Quentin, had just been making a resolute effort to devour one of the smaller snakes. As Quentin and his menagerie were an interruption to my interview with the Department of Justice, I suggested that he go into the next room, where four Congressmen were drearily waiting until I should be at leisure. I thought that he and his snakes would probably enliven their waiting time. He at once fell in with the suggestion and rushed up to the Congressmen with the assurance that he would there find kindred spirits. They at first thought the snakes were wooden ones, and there was some perceptible recoil when they realized that they were alive. Then the king snake went up Quentin's sleeve—he was three or four feet long—and we hesitated to drag him back because his scales rendered that difficult. The last I saw of Quentin, one Congressman was gingerly helping him off with his jacket, so as to let the snake crawl out of the upper end of the sleeve.

⤻

In the fall of 1907 the President made a tour through the West and South and went on a hunting-trip in Louisiana. In accordance with his unvarying custom he wrote regularly to his children while on his journeyings.

TRIALS OF A TRAVELLING PRESIDENT

On Board U. S. S. *Mississippi,* October 1, 1907.

DEAREST ETHEL:

The first part of my trip up to the time that we embarked on the river at Keokuk was just about in the ordinary style. I had continually to rush out to wave at the people at the towns through which the train passed. If the train stopped anywhere I had to make a very short speech to several hundred people who evidently thought they liked me, and whom I really liked, but to whom I had nothing in the world to say. At Canton and Keokuk I went through the usual solemn fes-tivities—the committee of reception and the guard of honor, with the open carriage, the lines of enthusiastic fellow-citizens to whom I bowed continually right and left, the speech which in each case I thought went off rather better than I had dared hope—for I felt as if I had spoken myself out. When I got on the boat, however, times grew easier. I still have to rush out continually, stand on the front part of the deck, and wave at groups of people on shore, and at stern-wheel steamboats draped with American flags and loaded with en-thusiastic excursionists. But I have a great deal of time to myself, and by gentle firmness I think I have succeeded in impressing on my good hosts that I rather resent allopathic doses of information about shoals and dykes, the amount of sand per cubic foot of water, the quantity of manufactures supplied by each river town, etc.

CHANGES OF THREE CENTURIES

On Board U. S. S. *Mississippi*, October I, 1907.

DEAR KERMIT:

.   .   .   .

After speaking at Keokuk this morning we got aboard this brand new stern-wheel steamer of the regular Mississippi type and started down-stream. I went up on the *Texas* and of course felt an almost irresistible desire to ask the pilot about Mark Twain. It is a broad, shallow, muddy river, at places the channel being barely wide enough for the boat to go through, though to my inexperienced eyes the whole river looks like a channel. The bottom lands, Illinois on one side and Missouri on the other, are sometimes overgrown with forests and sometimes great rich cornfields, with here and there a house, here and there villages, and now and then a little town. At every such place all the people of the neighborhood have gathered to greet me. The water-front of the towns would be filled with a dense packed mass of men, women, and children, waving flags. The little villages have not only their own population, but also the farmers who have driven in in their wagons with their wives and children from a dozen miles back—just such farmers as came to see you and the cavalry on your march through Iowa last summer.

It is my first trip on the Mississippi, and I am greatly interested in it. How wonderful in its rapidity of movement has been the history of our country, compared with the history of the old world. For untold ages this river had been flowing through the lonely continent, not very greatly changed since the close of the Pleistocene. During all these myriads of years the prairie and the forest came down to its banks. The immense herds of the buffalo and the elk wandered along them season after season, and the Indian hunters on foot or in canoes trudged along the banks or skimmed the water. Probably a thousand years saw no change that would have been noticeable to our eyes. Then three centuries ago began the work of change. For a century its effects were not perceptible. Just nothing but an occasional French fleet or wild half savage French-Canadian explorer passing up or down the river or one of its branches in an Indian canoe; then the first faint changes, the building of one or two little French fur traders' hamlets, the passing of one or two British officers' boats, and the very rare appearance of the uncouth American backwoodsman.

Then the change came with a rush. Our settlers reached the head-waters of the Ohio, and flatboats and keel-boats began to go down to the mouth of the Mississippi, and the Indians and the game they followed began their last great march to the west. For ages they had marched back and forth, but from this march there was never to be a return. Then the day of steamboat traffic began, and the growth of the first American cities and states along the river with their strength and their squalor and their raw pride. Then this mighty steamboat traffic passed its zenith and collapsed, and for a generation the river towns have dwindled compared with the towns which took their importance from the growth of the railroads. I think of it all as I pass down the river.

October 4. ... We are steaming down the river now between Tennessee and Arkansas. The forest comes down a little denser to the bank, the houses do not look quite so well kept; otherwise there is not much change. There are a dozen steamers accompanying us, filled with delegates from various river cities. The people are all out on the banks to greet us still. Moreover, at night, no matter what the hour is that we pass a town, it is generally illuminated, and sometimes whistles and noisy greetings, while our steamboats whistle in equally noisy response, so that our sleep is apt to be broken. Seventeen governors of different states are along, in a boat by themselves. I have seen a good deal of them, however, and it has been of real use to me, especially as regards two or three problems that are up. At St. Louis there was an enormous multitude of people out to see us. The procession was in a drenching rain, in which I stood bareheaded, smiling affably and waving my drowned hat to those hardy members of the crowd who declined to go to shelter. At Cairo, I was also greeted with great enthusiasm, and I was interested to find that there was still extreme bitterness felt over Dickens's description of the town and the people in "Martin Chuzzlewit" sixty-five years ago.

. . . .

PECULIARITIES OF MISSISSIPPI STEAMBOATS

On Board U. S. S. *Mississippi*, Oct. 1, 1907.

DEAR ARCHIE:

. . . .

I am now on what I believe will be my last trip of any consequence while I am President. Until I got to Keokuk, Iowa, it was about like any other trip, but it is now pleasant going down the Mississippi, though I admit that I would rather be at home. We are on a funny, stern-wheel steamer. Mr. John McIlhenny is with me, and Capt. Seth Bullock among others. We have seen wild geese and ducks and cormorants on the river, and the people everywhere come out in boats and throng or cluster on the banks to greet us.

October 4. You would be greatly amused at these steamboats, and I think you will like your trip up the Mississippi next spring, if only everything goes right, and Mother is able to make it. There is no hold to the boat, just a flat bottom with a deck, and on this deck a foot or so above the water stands the engine-room, completely open at the sides and all the machinery visible as you come up to the boat. Both ends are blunt, and the gangways are drawn up to big cranes. Of course the boats could not stand any kind of a sea, but here they are very useful, for they are shallow and do not get hurt when they bump into the bank or one another. The river runs down in a broad, swirling, brown current, and nobody but an expert could tell the channel. One pilot or another is up in the *Texas* all day long and all night. Now the channel goes close under one bank, then we have to cross the river and go under the other bank; then there will come a deep spot when we can go anywhere. Then we wind in and out among shoals and sand-bars. At night the steamers are all lighted up, for there are a dozen of them in company with us. It is nice to look back at them as they twist after us in a long winding line down the river.

THE LONE CAT OF THE CAMP

Stamboul, La., Oct. 13, 1907.

DARLING QUENTIN:

When we shifted camp we came down here and found a funny little wooden shanty, put up by some people who now and then come out here and sleep in it when they fish or shoot. The only living thing around it was a pussy-cat. She was most friendly and pleasant, and we found that she had been living here for two years. When people were in the neighborhood, she would take what scraps she could get, but the rest of the time she would catch her own game for herself. She was pretty thin when we came, and has already fattened visibly. She was not in the least disconcerted by the appearance of the hounds, and none of them paid the slightest attention to her when she wandered about among them. We are camped on the edge of a lake. This morning before breakfast I had a good swim in it, the water being warmer than the air, and this evening I rowed on it in the moonlight. Every night we hear the great owls hoot and laugh in uncanny fashion.

Camp on Tenesas Bayou, Oct. 6, 1907.

Darling Ethel:

Here we are in camp. It is very picturesque, and as comfortable as possible. We have a big fly tent for the horses; the hounds sleep with them, or with the donkeys! There is a white hunter, Ben Lily, who has just joined us, who is a really remarkable character. He literally lives in the woods. He joined us early this morning, with one dog. He had tramped for twenty-four hours through the woods, without food or water, and had slept a couple of hours in a crooked tree, like a wild turkey.

He has a mild, gentle face, blue eyes, and full beard; he is a religious fanatic, and is as hardy as a bear or elk, literally caring nothing for fatigue and exposure, which we couldn't stand at all. He doesn't seem to consider the 24 hours' trip he has just made, any more than I should a half hour's walk before breakfast. He quotes the preacher Talmage continually.

This is a black belt. The people are almost all negroes, curious creatures, some of them with Indian blood, like those in "Voodoo Tales." Yesterday we met two little negresses riding one mule, bare-legged, with a rope bridle.

Tenesas Bayou, Oct. 10, 1907.

BLESSED ARCHIE:

I just loved your letter. I was so glad to hear from you. I was afraid you would have trouble with your Latin. What a funny little fellow Opdyke* must be; I am glad you like him. How do you get on at football?

We have found no bear. I shot a deer; I sent a picture of it to Kermit.

A small boy here caught several wildcats. When one was in the trap he would push a box towards it, and it would itself get into it, to hide; and so he would capture it alive. But one, instead of getting into the box, combed the hair of the small boy!

We have a great many hounds in camp; at night they gaze solemnly into the fire.

*Leonard Opdyke, Groton School student in the class of 1914, one year behind Archie.

Dr. Lambert has caught a good many bass, which we have enjoyed at the camp table.

Bear Bayou, Oct. 16, 1907.

DARLING ARCHIE:

We have had no luck with the bear; but we have killed as many deer as we needed for meat, and the hounds caught a wildcat. Our camp is as comfortable as possible, and we have great camp fires at night.

One of the bear-hunting planters with me told me he once saw a bear, when overtaken by the hounds, lie down flat on its back with all its legs stretched out, while the dogs barked furiously all around it.

Suddenly the bear sat up with a jump, and frightened all the dogs so that they nearly turned back somersaults.

At this camp there is a nice tame pussy-cat which lies out here all the time, catching birds, mice, or lizards; but very friendly with any party of hunters which happens along.

P. S.—I have just killed a bear; I have written Kermit about it.

THE BEAR PLAYS DEAD

THE BEAR SITS UP

SHOOTING THE BEAR

En route to Washington, Oct. 22, 1907.

DEAR TED:

"Bad old father" is coming back after a successful trip. It was a success in every way, including the bear hunt; but in the case of the bear hunt we only just made it successful and no more, for it was not until the twelfth day of steady hunting that I got my bear. Then I shot it in the most approved hunter's style, going up on it in a canebrake as it made a walking bay before the dogs. I also killed a deer—more by luck than anything else, as it was a difficult shot.

QUENTIN'S "EXQUISITE JEST"

White House, Jan. 2, 1908.

DEAR ARCHIE:

Friday night Quentin had three friends, including the little Taft boy,* to spend the night with him. They passed an evening and night of delirious rapture, it being a continuous roughhouse save when they would fall asleep for an hour or two from sheer exhaustion. I interfered but once, and that was to stop an exquisite jest of Quentin's which consisted in procuring sulphureted hydrogen to be used on the other boys when they got into bed. They played hard, and it made me realize how old I had grown and how very busy I had been these last few years, to find that they had grown so that I was not needed in the play. Do you recollect how we all of us used to play hide-and-go-seek in the White House?

---

*Charlie Taft, son of Secretary of War William Howard Taft and one of Quentin's "White House Gang."

and have obstacle races down the hall when you brought in your friends?

Mother continues much attached to Scamp, who is certainly a cunning little dog. He is very affectionate, but so exceedingly busy when we are out on the grounds, that we only catch glimpses of him zigzagging at full speed from one end of the place to the other. The kitchen cat and he have strained relations but have not yet come to open hostility.

White House, Jan. 27, 1908.

DEAR ARCHIE:

Scamp is really a cunning little dog, but he takes such an extremely keen interest in hunting, and is so active, that when he is out on the grounds with us we merely catch glimpses of him as he flashes by. The other night after the Judicial Reception when we went up-stairs to supper the kitchen cat suddenly appeared parading down the hall with great friendliness, and was forthwith exiled to her proper home again.

TOM PINCH

White House, February 23, 1908.

DEAREST KERMIT:

I quite agree with you about Tom Pinch. He is a despicable kind of character; just the kind of character Dickens liked, because he had himself a thick streak of maudlin sentimentality of the kind that, as somebody phrased it, "made him wallow naked in the pathetic." It always interests me about Dickens to think how much first-class work he did and how almost all of it was mixed up with every kind of cheap, second-rate matter. I am very fond of him.

There are innumerable characters that he has created which symbolize vices, virtues, follies, and the like almost as well as the characters in Bunyan; and therefore I think the wise thing to do is simply to skip the bosh and twaddle and vulgarity and untruth, and get the benefit out of the rest. Of course one fundamental difference between Thackeray and Dickens is that Thackeray was a gentleman and Dickens was not. But a man might do some mighty good work and not be a gentleman in any sense.

"MARTIN CHUZZLEWIT"

White House, February 29, 1908.

DEAREST KERMIT:

Of course I entirely agree with you about "Martin Chuzzlewit." But the point seems to me that the preposterous perversion of truth and the ill-nature and malice of the book are of consequence chiefly as indicating Dickens' own character, about which I care not a rap; whereas, the characters in American shortcomings and vices and follies as typified are immortal, and, moreover, can be studied with great profit by all of us to-day. Dickens was an ill-natured, selfish cad and boor, who had no understanding of what the word gentleman meant, and no appreciation of hospitality or good treatment. He was utterly incapable of seeing the high purpose and the real greatness which (in spite of the presence also of much that was bad or vile) could have been visible all around him here in America to any man whose vision was both keen and lofty. He could not see the qualities of the young men growing up here, though it was these qualities that enabled these men to conquer the West and to fight to a finish the great Civil War, and though they were to produce leadership like that of Lincoln, Lee, and Grant. Naturally he would think there was no gentleman in New York, because by no possibility could he have recognized a gentleman if he had met one. Naturally he would condemn all America because he had not the soul to see what America was really doing. But he was in his element in describing with bitter truthfulness Scadder and Jefferson Brick, and Elijah Pogram, and Hannibal Chollup, and Mrs. Hominy and the various other characters, great and small, that have always made me enjoy "Martin Chuzzlewit." Most of these characters we still have with us.

GOOD READING FOR PACIFISTS

March 4, 1908.

DEAREST KERMIT:

You have recently been writing me about Dickens. Senator Lodge gave me the following first-class quotation from a piece by Dickens about "Proposals for Amusing Posterity":

"And I would suggest that if a body of gentlemen possessing their full phrenological share of the combative and antagonistic organs, could only be induced to form themselves into a society for Declaiming about Peace, with a very considerable war-whoop against all non-declaimers; and if they could only be prevailed upon to sum up eloquently the many unspeakable miseries and horrors of War, and to present them to their own country as a conclusive reason for its being undefended against War, and becoming a prey of the first despot who might choose to inflict those miseries and horrors—why then I really believe we should have got to the very best joke we could hope to have in our whole Complete Jest-Book for Posterity and might fold our arms and rest convinced that we had done enough for that discerning Patriarch's amusement."

This ought to be read before all the tomfool peace societies and anti-imperialist societies of the present-day.

QUENTIN AS A BALL-PLAYER

White House, March 8, 1908.

DEAREST ARCHIE:

Yesterday morning Quentin brought down all his Force School baseball nine to practise on the White House grounds. It was great fun to see them, and Quentin made a run. It reminded me of when you used to come down with the Friend's School eleven. Moreover, I was reminded of the occasional rows in the eleven by an outburst in connection with the nine which resulted in their putting off of it a small boy who Quentin assured me was the "meanest kid in town." I like to see Quentin practicing baseball. It gives me hopes that one of my boys will not take after his father in this respect, and will prove able to play the national game!

Ethel has a delightful new dog—a white bull terrier—not much more than a puppy as yet. She has named it Mike and it seems very affectionate. Scamp is really an extraordinary ratter, and kills a great many rats in the White House, in the cellars and on the lower floor and among the machinery. He is really a very nice little dog.

White House, March 15, 1908.

DEAREST ARCHIE:

Quentin is now taking a great interest in baseball. Yesterday the Force School nine, on which he plays second base, played the P Street nine on the White House grounds where Quentin has marked out a diamond. The Force School nine was victorious by a score of 22 to 5. I told Quentin I was afraid the P Street boys must have felt badly and he answered, "Oh, I guess not; you see I filled them up with lemonade afterward!"

Charlie Taft is on his nine.

Did you hear of the dreadful time Ethel had with her new bull terrier, Mike? She was out riding with Fitz Lee, who was on Roswell, and Mike was following. They suppose that Fidelity must have accidentally kicked Mike. The first they knew the bulldog sprang at the little mare's throat. She fought pluckily, rearing and plunging, and shook him off, and then Ethel galloped away. As soon as she halted, Mike overtook her and attacked Fidelity again. He seized her by the shoulder and tried to seize her by the throat, and twice Ethel had to break away and gallop off, Fitz Lee endeavoring in vain to catch the dog. Finally he succeeded, just as Mike had got Fidelity by the hock. He had to give Mike a tremendous beating to restore him to obedience; but of course Mike will have to be disposed of. Fidelity was bitten in several places and it was a wonder that Ethel was able to keep her seat, because naturally the frightened little mare reared and plunged and ran.

FOUR SHEEPISH SMALL BOYS

White House, April 11, 1908.

DEAREST ARCHIE:

Ethel has bought on trial an eight-months bull-dog pup. He is very cunning, very friendly, and wriggles all over in a frantic desire to be petted.

Quentin really seems to be getting on pretty well with his baseball. In each of the last two games he made a base hit and a run. I have just had to give him and three of his associates a dressing down—one of the three being Charlie Taft. Yesterday afternoon was rainy, and four of them played five hours inside the White House. They were very boisterous and were all the time on the verge of mischief, and finally they made spit-balls and deliberately put them on the portraits. I did not discover it until after dinner, and then pulled Quentin out of bed and had him take them all off the portraits, and this morning required him to bring in the three other culprits before me. I explained to them that they had acted like boors; that it would have been a disgrace to have behaved so in any gentleman's house; that Quentin could have no friend to see him, and the other three could not come inside the White House, until I felt that a sufficient time had elapsed to serve as punishment. They were four very sheepish small boys when I got through with them.

JOHN BURROUGHS AND THE FLYING SQUIRRELS

White House, May 10, 1908.

DEAREST ARCHIE:

Mother and I had great fun at Pine Knot. Mr. Burroughs,* whom I call Oom John, was with us and we greatly enjoyed having him. But one night he fell into great disgrace! The flying squirrels that were there last Christmas had raised a brood, having built a large nest inside of the room in which you used to sleep and in which John Burroughs slept. Of course they held high carnival at night-time. Mother and I do not mind them at all, and indeed

*John Burroughs, well-known naturalist. "Oom John" means "Uncle John" in Dutch.

rather like to hear them scrambling about, and then as a sequel to a sudden frantic fight between two of them, hearing or seeing one little fellow come plump down to the floor and scuttle off again to the wall. But one night they waked up John Burroughs and he spent a misguided hour hunting for the nest, and when he found it took it down and caught two of the young squirrels and put them in a basket. The next day under Mother's direction I took them out, getting my fingers somewhat bitten in the process, and loosed them in our room, where we had previously put back the nest. I do not think John Burroughs profited by his misconduct, because the squirrels were more active than ever that night both in his room and ours, the disturbance in their family affairs having evidently made them restless!

BEAUTY OF WHITE HOUSE GROUNDS

White House, May 17, 1908.

DEAREST ARCHIE:

Quentin is really doing pretty well with his baseball, and he is perfectly absorbed in it. He now occasionally makes a base hit if the opposing pitcher is very bad; and his nine wins more than one-half of its games.

The grounds are too lovely for anything, and spring is here, or rather early summer, in full force. Mother's flower-gardens are now as beautiful as possible, and the iron railings of the fences south of them are covered with clematis and roses in bloom. The trees are in full foliage and the grass brilliant green, and my friends, the warblers, are trooping to the north in full force.

QUENTIN AND A BEEHIVE

White House, May 30, 1908.

DEAREST ARCHIE:

Quentin has met with many adventures this week; in spite of the fact that he has had a bad cough which has tended to interrupt the variety of his career. He has become greatly interested in bees, and the other day started down to get a beehive from somewhere, being accompanied by a mongrel looking small boy as to whose name I inquired. When repeated by Quentin it was obviously an Italian name. I asked who he was and Quentin responded: "Oh, his father keeps a fruit-stand." However, they got their bees all right and Quentin took the hive up to a school exhibit. There some of the bees got out and were left behind ("Poor homeless miserables," as Quentin remarked of them), and yesterday they at intervals added great zest to life in the classroom. The hive now reposes in the garden and Scamp surveys it for hours at a time with absorbed interest. After a while he will get to investigating it, and then he will find out more than he expects to.

This afternoon Quentin was not allowed to play ball because of his cough, so he was keeping the score when a foul tip caught him in the eye. It was quite a bad blow, but Quentin was very plucky about it and declined to go in until the game was finished, an hour or so later. By that time his eye had completely shut up and he now has a most magnificent bandage around his head over that eye, and feels much like a baseball hero. I came in after dinner to take a look at him and to my immense amusement found that he was lying flat on his back in bed saying his prayers, while Mademoiselle was kneeling down. It took me a moment or two to grasp the fact that good Mademoiselle wished to impress on him that it was not right to say his prayers unless he knelt down, and as that in this case he could not kneel down she would do it in his place!

QUENTIN AND TURNER
(To Mrs. Nicholas Longworth, Cincinnati, Ohio)

Oyster Bay, June 29, 1908.

. . . .

Quentin is really too funny for anything. He got his legs fearfully sunburned the other day, and they blistered, became inflamed, and ever-faithful Mother had to hold a clinic on him. Eyeing his blistered and scarlet legs, he remarked, "They look like a Turner sunset, don't they?" And then, after a pause, "I won't be caught again this way! quoth the raven, 'Nevermore!' " I was not surprised at his quoting Poe, but I would like to know where the ten-year-old scamp picked up any knowledge of Turner's sunsets.

QUENTIN AND THE PIG

White House, October 17, 1908.

DEAREST KERMIT:

. . . .

Quentin performed a characteristic feat yesterday. He heard that Schmidt, the animal man, wanted a small pig, and decided that he would turn an honest penny by supplying the want. So out in the neighborhood of his school he called on an elderly darkey who, he had seen, possessed little pigs; bought one; popped it into a bag; astutely dodged the school—having a well-founded distrust of how the boys would feel toward his passage with the pig—and took the car for home. By that time the pig had freed itself from the bag, and, as he explained, he journeyed in with a "small squealish pig" under his arm; but as the conductor was a friend of his he was not put off. He bought it for a dollar and sold it to Schmidt for a dollar and a quarter, and feels as if he had found a permanent line of business. Schmidt then festooned it in red ribbons and sent it to parade the streets. I gather that Quentin led it around for part of the parade, but he was somewhat vague on this point, evidently being a little uncertain as to our approval of the move.

A PRESIDENTIAL FALL

White House, Nov. 8, 1908.

DEAREST ARCHIE:

Quentin is getting along very well; he plays centre on his football eleven, and in a match for juniors in tennis he got into the semifinals. What is more important, he seems to be doing very well with his studies, and to get on well with the boys, and is evidently beginning to like the school. He has shown himself very manly. Kermit is home now, and is a perfect dear.

The other day while taking a scramble walk over Rock Creek, when I came to that smooth-face of rock which we get round by holding on to the little bit of knob that we call the Button, the top of this button came off between my thumb and forefinger. I hadn't supposed that I was putting much weight on it, but evidently I was, for I promptly lost my balance, and finding I was falling, I sprang out into the creek. There were big rocks in it, and the water was rather shallow, but I landed all right and didn't hurt myself the least bit in the world.

MORE ABOUT QUENTIN

White House, Nov. 22, 1908.

DEAREST ARCHIE:

I handed your note and the two dollar bill to Quentin, and he was perfectly delighted. It came in very handy, because poor Quentin has been in bed with his leg in a plaster cast, and the two dollars I think went to make up a fund with which he purchased a fascinating little steam-engine, which has been a great source of amusement to him. He is out to-day visiting some friends, although his leg is still in a cast. He has a great turn for mechanics.

White House, Nov. 27, 1908.

BLESSED ARCHIE:

It is fine to hear from you and to know you are having a good time. Quentin, I am happy to say, is now thoroughly devoted to his school. He feels that he is a real Episcopal High School boy, and takes the keenest interest in everything. Yesterday, Thanksgiving Day, he had various friends here. His leg was out of plaster and there was nothing he did not do. He roller-skated; he practised football; he had engineering work and electrical work; he went all around the city; he romped all over the White House; he went to the slaughter-house and got a pig for Thanksgiving dinner.

Ethel is perfectly devoted to Ace, who adores her. The other day he was lost for a little while; he had gone off on a side street and unfortunately saw a cat in a stable and rushed in and killed it, and they had him tied up there when one of our men found him.

In a way I know that Mother misses Scamp, but in another way she does not, for now all the squirrels are very tame and cunning and are hopping about the lawn and down on the paths all the time, so that we see them whenever we walk, and they are not in the least afraid of us.

White House, Dec. 3, 1908.

DEAREST ARCHIE:

I have a very strong presentiment that Santa Claus will not forget that watch! Quentin went out shooting with Dr. Rixey on Monday and killed three rabbits, which I think was pretty good. He came back very dirty and very triumphant, and Mother, feeling just as triumphant, brought him promptly over with his gun and his three rabbits to see me in the office. On most days now he rides out to school, usually on Achilles. Very shortly he will begin to spend his nights at the school, however. He has become sincerely attached to the school, and at the moment thinks he would rather stay there than go to Groton; but this is a thought he will get over—with Mother's active assistance. He has all kinds of friends, including some who are on a hockey team with him here in the city. The hockey team apparently plays hockey now and then, but only very occasionally, and spends most of the time disciplining its own members.

In 1909, after retiring from the Presidency, Colonel Roosevelt went on a hunting trip in Africa, writing as usual to his children while away.

TRIBUTE TO KERMIT

On the 'Nzor River, Nov. 13, 1909.

DARLING ETHEL:

Here we are, by a real tropical river, with game all around, and no human being within several days' journey. At night the hyenas come round the camp, uttering their queer howls; and once or twice we have heard lions; but unfortunately have never seen them. Kermit killed a leopard yesterday. He has really done so very well! It is rare for a boy with his refined tastes and his genuine appreciation of literature—and of so much else—to be also an exceptionally bold and hardy sportsman. He is still altogether too reckless; but by my hen-with-one-chicken attitude, I think I shall get him out of Africa uninjured; and his keenness, cool nerve, horsemanship, hardihood, endurance, and good eyesight make him a really good wilderness hunter. We have become genuinely attached to Cuninghame* and Tarlton,† and all three naturalists, especially Heller‡ and also to our funny black attendants. The porters always amuse us; at this moment about thirty of them are bringing in the wood for the camp fires, which burn all night; and they are all chanting in chorus, the chant being nothing but the words *"Wood—plenty of wood to burn!"*

A Merry Christmas to you! And to Archie and Quentin. How I

---

*R. J. Cuninghame, a Scot and a Cambridge man, outstanding hunter-naturalist and longtime resident of Africa who had charge of TR's safari.

†Leslie J. Tarlton of Nairobi, an Australian and a famous hunter who served through the South African war.

‡Edmund Heller, one of the naturalists chosen by the Smithsonian Institution to accompany TR on his African safari. The other two were Edgar A. Mearns and J. Alden Loring. In 1934 Heller and TR were coauthors of *Life-Histories of African Game Animals*, two volumes.

wish I were to be with you all, no matter how cold it might be at Sagamore; but I suppose we shall be sweltering under mosquito nets in Uganda.

LONGING FOR HOME

Campalla, Dec. 23, 1909.

BLESSEDEST ETHELY-BYE:

Here we are, the most wise Bavian—particularly nice—and the Elderly Parent, on the last stage of their journey. I am enjoying it all, but I think Kermit regards me as a little soft, because I am so eagerly looking forward to the end, when I shall see darling, pretty Mother, my own sweetheart, and the very nicest of all nice daughters—you blessed girlie. Do you remember when you explained, with some asperity, that of course you wished Ted were at home, because you didn't have anybody as a really intimate companion, whereas Mother had "old Father"? It is a *great* comfort to have a daughter to whom I can write about all kinds of intimate things!

This is a most interesting place. We crossed the great Nyanza Lake, in a comfortable steamer, in 24 hours, seeing a lovely sunset across the vast expanse of waters; and the moonlight later was as lovely. Here it is as hot as one would expect directly on the Equator, and the brilliant green landscape is fairly painted with even more brilliant flowers, on trees, bush, and vines; while the strange, semi-civilized people are most interesting. The queer little king's Prime Minister, an exceedingly competent, gorgeously dressed, black man, reminds Kermit of a rather civilized Umslopagaar—if that is the way you spell Rider Haggard's Zulu hero.

In this little native town we are driven round in rickshaws, each with four men pushing and pulling, who utter a queer, clanging note of exclamation in chorus, every few seconds, hour after hour.

THE LAST HUNT

Gondokoro, Feb. 27, 1910.

DEAREST ARCHIE:

Here, much to my pleasure, I find your letter written after the snow-storm at Sagamore. No snow here! On two or three days the thermometer at noon has stood at 115 degrees in the shade. All three naturalists and Mr. Cuninghame, the guide, have been sick, and so Kermit and I made our last hunt alone, going for eight days into the Lado. We were very successful, getting among other things three giant eland, which are great prizes. We worked hard; Kermit of course worked hardest, for he is really a first-class walker and runner; I had to go slowly, but I kept at it all day and every day. Kermit has really become not only an excellent hunter but also a responsible and trustworthy man, fit to lead; he managed the whole caravan and after hunting all day he would sit up half the night taking care of the skins. He is also the nicest possible companion. We are both very much attached to our gunbearers and tent boys, and will be sorry to part with them.

QUENTIN GROWN-UP

New York, Dec. 23, 1911.

DEAR ARCHIE:

Quentin turned up last night. He is half an inch taller than I am, and is in great shape. He is much less fat than he was, and seems to be turning out right in every way. I was amused to have him sit down and play the piano pretty well. We miss you dreadfully now that Christmas has come. The family went into revolt about my slouch hat, which Quentin christened "Old Mizzoura," and so I have had to buy another with a less pronounced crown and brim. We all drank your good health at dinner.

EPILOGUE

THEODORE ROOSEVELT
(1858–1919)

The ten years remaining of Father's life after leaving the White House in 1909 were in no sense a "retirement." After an exciting safari in Africa with Kermit, and a triumphant tour of the capitals of Europe with Edith, Ethel, and Kermit, TR returned to the turbulence of American politics. Unhappy with President Taft, TR formed his own Progressive ("Bull Moose") party and made an unsuccessful bid for the presidency in 1912. He continued to write and, at the end of his life, had more than twenty books to his credit, not to mention more than 150,000 letters. He and Kermit teamed up again on an exploring expedition of an unknown Brazilian river, a trip that seriously impaired his health and which almost ended in his death. He had eight grandchildren on whom he lavished affection in his "capacity as natural-born grandfather." He was an early and ardent advocate of his country's entrance into World War I. Trying unsuccessfully to enlist himself, he proudly watched Ethel and his four sons head overseas and suffered the loss of Quentin with anguished stoicism. Archie, who had been wounded, was home on leave when his father died in his sleep at Sagamore Hill on January 6, 1919. "The old lion is dead," he cabled his brothers in Germany. Father was sixty years old.

EDITH KERMIT ROOSEVELT
(1861–1948)

Mother lived on in the big house at Sagamore Hill for twenty-nine years after Father's death. She remained a private person, except for occasional appearances at events that perpetuated TR's memory or on behalf of Republican causes. She traveled extensively to all four quarters of the globe in the early years, often with members of the family. When age forced her to curtail her voyages, she unexpectedly bought a large house in Brooklyn, Connecticut, where her Tyler ancestors had once lived and where she elected to spend her remaining summers. Ted, Kermit, Ethel, and Archie all had homes in or near Oyster Bay, so at Sagamore she was surrounded by large numbers of grandchildren. Unlike TR, however, her enthusiasm for them was muted. "I like to see their little faces," she would say, "but I prefer to see their backs."

ALICE ROOSEVELT LONGWORTH
(1884–1980)

First of TR's children to be born and last to die, "Princess Alice" remained an irreverent and daunting figure on the political and social scene of Washington. Her husband, Nicholas Longworth, eventually became speaker of the House before he died in 1931. But it was Alice who was always the celebrity. She gave birth to her only child, Paulina, in her forty-first year and, after Paulina's death at thirty-one, won custody of her sole grandchild, Joanna, with whom she lived until her own death at ninety-six. Widely known as "Washington's other monument," she was acquainted with every president from Benjamin Harrison to Gerald Ford, some of whom she admired, many of whom she did not, but most of whom were in awe of her and her injunction "If you can't say something good about someone, sit right here by me."

THEODORE ROOSEVELT, JR.
(1887–1944)

Although Ted was discouraged from going to West Point and becoming a professional soldier, he served valiantly in both world
wars, and won the Congressional Medal of Honor as a brigadier
general in World War II. Ted also served in the New York State
Assembly and as assistant secretary of the Navy, like his father, but
was defeated for governor of New York by Al Smith in 1924. He
was governor of Puerto Rico, 1929–1932, and governor general of
the Philippines, 1932–1933. Ted was the author of eight books,
and became vice president of Doubleday Doran, the publishing
firm. He married Eleanor Butler Alexander in 1910 and had four
children, including Theodore Roosevelt III and Quentin II. They
built a family home, Old Orchard, on the grounds of Sagamore
Hill. He died of a heart attack in France on July 12, 1944, some
days after leading the first assault wave on D day. By family tradition, Roosevelts are buried where they fall. Ted lies in Normandy.

KERMIT ROOSEVELT
(1889–1943)

Of the brothers, Kermit was the one who most shared his father's enthusiasm for out-of-door sport. Having accompanied TR on two major hunting and exploring expeditions in Africa and Brazil, he continued to indulge his passion for life in the wild in Asia, Alaska, the Galápagos Islands, and the East and West Indies and became, at home, president of the Audubon Society. He founded the Roosevelt Steamship Company and organized the United States Lines. He served in the British Army in both world wars before the United States entry, and then transferred to the American Army. He married Belle Wyatt Willard, daughter of the U.S. ambassador to Spain, in Madrid in June 1914. Father of four children and fifty years of age, he nonetheless insisted on enlisting in World War II. Tragically, Kermit had over the years suffered increasingly from alcoholism and depression. He killed himself while on active service in Alaska and was buried there under the frozen tundra.

ETHEL ROOSEVELT DERBY
(1891–1977)

Ethel married a longtime friend and admirer, Dr. Richard Derby, in 1913 and, a year later as a nurse, accompanied her surgeon husband to France to work at the American Ambulance Hospital, becoming the first of TR's children to serve in the war zone. Her close involvement with the American Red Cross began then and continued until her death. She raised her four children, one of whom died in childhood, in Oyster Bay and was a leader in countless local church and community activities. Fondly known as the "First Lady of Oyster Bay," she led the movement to preserve Sagamore Hill after Edith's death and was a loyal member of the Theodore Roosevelt Association, dedicated to the memory of TR. "They may have a 'princess' in Washington," the locals said, referring to Alice, "but we have a queen in Oyster Bay."

ARCHIBALD BULLOCH ROOSEVELT

(1894–1979)

Like his brothers, Archie enlisted in World War I and distinguished himself as a company commander in the American Expeditionary Force in France. Wounded three times, he was awarded the Croix de Guerre as he lay on the operating table. Again like his brothers, at forty-nine he persuaded the Army to let him go into active combat in World War II, from which he returned a wounded hero and was awarded the Silver Star with Oak Leaf Cluster. He had a lifelong career in the financial world, forming Roosevelt & Weigold, later Roosevelt & Cross, a firm specializing in tax-exempt bonds. Archie married Grace Stackpole Lockwood in 1917 and had four children.

QUENTIN ROOSEVELT
(1897–1918)

Quentin had entered Harvard, class of 1919, when war broke out, and he left in 1916 to train as an aviator. He had become engaged to a beautiful young woman, Flora Whitney, before he sailed for France in July of 1917. Continuing his training abroad until the following June, he was then sent to the front with the Ninety-fifth Air Squadron. On July 11 he got his first Boche. Three days later, while on an early patrol with three others, they were attacked by seven Fokkers. Quentin "gave them a hot fight," as the Harvard Roll of Honor reported. His opponent counted twenty bullet holes in his machine, but Quentin was at too great a disadvantage. "He was shot through the head and fell at Chemery, a little village near the Marne." The Germans buried him where he crashed, but after World War II his remains were moved to Normandy, where he lies in an American military cemetery next to his brother Ted.

ACKNOWLEDGMENTS
AND SOURCES

David McCullough not only wrote the foreword to this book; some years ago he introduced me to the remarkable man Theodore Roosevelt and to his *Letters to His Children,* and he has encouraged and guided me on this project ever since. Having five children of his own and a devotion to his wife and family much like TR's, David McCullough traced with great sensitivity Roosevelt's early life in his book *Mornings on Horseback,* which stressed the close bonds between young Theodore and his parents—in particular his father. My debt to him is incalculable.

Early on I consulted my old friend Elting E. Morison, who to my great sorrow died before this book was completed. With John M. Blum, Elting Morison edited the eight-volume *The Letters of Theodore Roosevelt,* a prime source for this and so many other books about TR. At a later date I talked with John Blum, and I owe much to both of these scholars for their insights.

Dr. John Allen Gable, executive director of the Theodore Roosevelt Association, and Wallace F. Dailey, curator of the Theodore Roosevelt Collection at Harvard University, were unfailingly cour-

teous and helpful over the course of my visits and telephone conversations. My thanks to them, and to Kathleen Young of the Sagamore Hill National Historic Site and Joan Harris of the Theodore
Roosevelt Birthplace.

Although none of the surviving members of the current Roosevelt clan are old enough to remember TR firsthand, they generously shared with me what mementos they did have and made
suggestions of leads to follow. I am especially indebted to TR's
granddaughters Edith Roosevelt Williams and Sarah Alden
Gannett, daughters of Ethel Roosevelt Derby; to his great-grand-
daughter Joanna Sturm, Alice Roosevelt Longworth's granddaughter; to P. James Roosevelt, grandson of two of TR's first cousins,
W. Emlen Roosevelt and John E. Roosevelt; and to Evan Cowles,
great-grandson of TR's sister Anna.

My thanks also to Selwa Roosevelt, J. Willard Roosevelt,
Theodore Roosevelt IV, and Tweed Roosevelt; and to the many
others who helped in varying degrees, including Winthrop Aldrich,
Mary Louise Brewster, Matthew J. Bruccoli, Douglas Brown, John
W. Chanler, William A. Chanler, Henry A. Chauncey, Jr., William
G. Farrell, VMD, Philip Kerr, John and Janet Lawrence, Henry
Lee, Mary Alice Leonhardt, Nacky Loeb, Daniel Tyler Moore,
Katharine J. Owre, Margaret Slawson, and Michael Teague.

Fortunately, TR and a number of his family members wrote
books about their lives and I have relied on these, in particular,
TR's *Autobiography*, the eight volumes of *Letters*, his *Letters to Kermit*
(and the splendid Biographical Index prepared by the late Nora E.
Cordingly, which has been invaluable in annotating the *Letters to His
Children*), and his *Letters to Bamie*.

Edith Kermit Roosevelt kept "The Baby's Journal" to record her
children's early days. Excerpts from her letters to TR and to her sis-

ter, Emily, are from the Harvard College Library's Theodore Roosevelt Collection and are quoted by permission of the Houghton Library of Harvard University, as are the letters from Anna Roosevelt Cowles to her son, Sheffield.

Alice Roosevelt Longworth not only wrote her own autobiography, *Crowded Hours,* but has also been the subject of several lively biographies, notably *Mrs. L* by Michael Teague and *Princess Alice* by James Brough.

Theodore Roosevelt, Jr.'s *All in the Family,* describing the early life of the young Roosevelts, was particularly helpful, as was his brother Kermit's account of expeditions with his father in *Happy Hunting Grounds.*

Cousin Nicholas Roosevelt, a great admirer of TR's, occupied a unique position to observe the family next door. His book, *Theodore Roosevelt: The Man as I Knew Him,* offers many revealing glimpses.

In addition to family accounts, three books and one study about the Roosevelts were especially pertinent. First and foremost, Hermann Hagedorn's *The Roosevelt Family of Sagamore Hill* was a delightful and essential source. *The White House Gang* by Earle Looker, one of its members, captured life in the executive mansion when Quentin ruled the roost. The fine biography *Edith Kermit Roosevelt* by Sylvia Morris shed light on the family's life from the mother's perspective. Lastly, the historic resource study "Sagamore Hill and the Roosevelt Family" by Francis Wilshin, published by the National Park Service, provided an excellent summary of the years covered by this book.

Help during periods of research away from home can take many forms. Not the least of these is providing a hot meal, a comfortable bed, and a willing ear. To my old friends Mary Janney in Washington, D.C., and Rosalie Kerr in Belmont, Massachusetts, I am truly grateful for all the above and more.

After the research comes the writing, followed as is night the day by the editor's scalpel. As wielded by Robert Loomis, I have enjoyed the best, and it was a pleasure to see a master editor at work. My thanks to him cannot be measured.

I appreciate too the meticulous copyediting of Margaret Wimberger and the book design by Lilly Langotsky.

In my husband, the legendary publisher Chester Kerr, I have had both a sympathetic critic and a staunch supporter, a rare combination for which I am eternally thankful.

ABOUT THE EDITOR

JOAN PATERSON KERR was co-editor of *American Album*, published by American Heritage, and *The Romantic Egoists*, a pictorial history of Scott and Zelda Fitzgerald. She was also a picture editor at Newsweek Books and of the Book-of-the-Month Club series "The American Past." She lives in New Haven with her husband, publisher Chester Kerr.

ABOUT THE TYPE

This book was set in Centaur, a typeface designed by the American typographer Bruce Rogers in 1929. Centaur was a typeface that Rogers adapted from the fifteenth-century type of Nicholas Jenson and modified in 1948 for a cutting by the Monotype Corporation.